Kishwaukee College Library
21193 Malta Road
Malta, IL 60150-9699

At Issue

Should the Legal Drinking Age Be Lowered?

Milwaukee College Library
2493 Malta Road
Malta, Il 80150-9699

Other Books in the At Issue Series:

...kee College Library
21155 ... Road
Malta, IL 60150-...

At Issue

Should the Legal Drinking Age Be Lowered?

Stefan Kiesbye, Book Editor

GREENHAVEN PRESS
A part of Gale, Cengage Learning

GALE
CENGAGE Learning

Detroit • New York • San Francisco • New Haven, Conn • Waterville, Maine • London

Christine Nasso, *Publisher*
Elizabeth Des Chenes, *Managing Editor*

© 2008 Greenhaven Press, a part of Gale, Cengage Learning.

Gale and Greenhaven Press are registered trademarks used herein under license.

For more information, contact:
Greenhaven Press
27500 Drake Rd.
Farmington Hills, MI 48331-3535
Or you can visit our Internet site at gale.cengage.com

ALL RIGHTS RESERVED.
No part of this work covered by the copyright herein may be reproduced, transmitted, stored, or used in any form or by any means graphic, electronic, or mechanical, including but not limited to photocopying, recording, scanning, digitizing, taping, Web distribution, information networks, or information storage and retrieval systems, except as permitted under Section 107 or 108 of the 1976 United States Copyright Act, without the prior written permission of the publisher.

For product information and technology assistance, contact us at

Gale Customer Support, 1-800-877-4253
For permission to use material from this text or product, submit all requests online at
www.cengage.com/permissions

Further permissions questions can be emailed to permissionrequest@cengage.com

Articles in Greenhaven Press anthologies are often edited for length to meet page requirements. In addition, original titles of these works are changed to clearly present the main thesis and to explicitly indicate the author's opinion. Every effort is made to ensure that Greenhaven Press accurately reflects the original intent of the authors. Every effort has been made to trace the owners of copyrighted material.

Cover photograph reproduced by permission of Images.com/Corbis.

LIBRARY OF CONGRESS CATALOGING-IN-PUBLICATION DATA

Should the legal drinking age be lowered? / Stefan Kiesbye, book editor.
   p. cm. -- (At issue)
  Includes bibliographical references and index.
  ISBN-13: 978-0-7377-3934-3 (hardcover)
  ISBN-13: 978-0-7377-3935-0 (pbk.)
  1. Teenagers--Alcohol use--United States. 2. Alcoholism--United States.
  3. Drinking age--Law and legislation--United States. I. Kiesbye, Stefan.
  HV5135.S57 2008
  363.4'1--dc22
                                          2008004492

Printed in the United States of America
1 2 3 4 5   12 11 10 09 08
ED102

Contents

Introduction

A fter Prohibition in the United States ended in 1933, most states designated twenty-one as the minimum legal drinking age (MLDA). In the early seventies though, when the minimum age for voting was lowered to eighteen, twenty-nine states also lowered the MLDA to eighteen, nineteen, or twenty. Soon thereafter, studies found that car accidents, which had already been the leading cause of teenage fatalities, had increased.

Advocacy groups lobbied to restore the MLDA to twenty-one and were successful in many states. In 1984, Congress—concerned about the inconsistent state laws and fearing that teenagers would cross state borders to drink alcohol and increase traffic fatalities—passed the Uniform Drinking Age Act. It requires all states to enforce an MLDA of twenty-one or forfeit federal highway funding. President Ronald Reagan, after initial resistance, signed the bill into law on June 13.

At first glance, the Uniform Drinking Age Act looks like a success story. Alcohol-related traffic deaths have undeniably decreased since the mid-1980s, as many studies have shown. Mothers Against Drunk Driving (MADD), Students Against Destructive Decisions (SADD), and others claim that the legal drinking age works to keep teenagers alive. Any attempt to lower the legal drinking age, they say, will only lead to more traffic accidents and more deaths.

In recent years, however, this assumption has been heavily criticized by various groups and individuals. Opponents of the mandatory drinking age argue that better safety and drug abuse education has led to more responsible alcohol use as well as a decline in traffic deaths. They also credit new vehicle safety features—from car design to air bags—and seat belt laws for improved statistics.

Looking beyond traffic statistics, the question arises whether the existing laws are effective enough. In November 1998, University of Michigan junior Bradley McCue died after a night of celebrating his twenty-first birthday. That night, McCue drank twenty-four shots within 120 minutes, which left him with a lethal blood alcohol concentration (BAC) of .44. In Michigan, a person is considered drunk with a BAC of .10. None of the friends and peers who celebrated with him intervened.

Gary DeVercelly, an eighteen-year-old business administration student at New Jersey's Rider University, died in spring 2007 after he had fallen unconscious in a fraternity house after drinking three-quarters of a bottle of vodka within fifteen minutes. He was in a state of cardiac arrest and was briefly revived, but died in the hospital two days later.

While these examples seem to underline how dangerous drinking is for teenagers and young adults, making an argument for the existing MLDA, professors David Hanson and Roderic Park disagree. Park, a longtime college administrator, proposes "learner's permits" for underage persons "as a way to help teach moderate drinking and reduce alcohol abuse." He claims that:

> the minimum drinking age of 21 is not working. Recent national surveys show that about 90 percent of U.S. high school students have consumed alcohol beverages. Half of these teenagers drink regularly. These are "inexperienced" drinkers who have generally received no education on the personal and social consequences of alcohol abuse and are typically acting without parental knowledge or guidance.

Instead of learning how to drink responsibly, underage persons are driven underground, where alcohol consumption can have fatal consequences. Park contends that young adults:

> can legally purchase and drink alcohol only when they reach the arbitrary age of 21. There is no educational requirement

before they can legally purchase, such as knowledge of legal limitations and liabilities, the facts of intoxication, or the role of intoxication in the transmission of sexually transmitted diseases. There is no reason to assume that people suddenly and magically become mature or wise or thoughtful at any arbitrary age. Nevertheless, in a kind of simplistic hypocrisy, the age of 21 law has become part of our culture's "solution" to the problem of irresponsible drinking.

Park proposes a learner's permit similar to a driver's permit. After passing a course on responsible drinking and the consequences of alcohol abuse, the underage person would be issued a permit, allowing that person to consume alcoholic beverages under the supervision of parents or guardians. Park concedes that there is no guarantee that a permit will work, but says that "the point is to seek creative and workable solutions to the tragic consequences of alcohol abuse in American society."

The best method for eliminating these tragic consequences will likely be debated for years to come. The authors of *At Issue: Should the Legal Drinking Age Be Lowered?* address the benefits and consequences of lowering the drinking age and offer their solutions on the topic.

1

Alcohol Use in Twentieth-Century America

Mack P. Holt

Mack P. Holt is a professor of history at George Mason University.

With the rise of industrialism and urban cultures, many Americans were introduced to leisurely alcohol consumption. The alcohol prohibition from 1920 to 1930 followed many state initiatives outlawing the production of alcoholic beverages. Yet it had adverse consequences, such as hard liquor's replacing beer as the beverage of choice, and the creation of drinking as a rebellious—and therefore chic and glamorous—act. The post-Prohibition era saw the rise of the alcoholism-as-disease concept, and the widespread acceptance of drinking especially among women. Drinking, helped by advertising, rose until the 1980s, when a new health consciousness started the trend toward moderation and sobriety.

Drinking entered the twentieth century a fiercely contested act. As a result of seventy-five years of temperance advocacy, few respectable publications dared to show drink in a positive light, and the same was true of the fledgling film industry. Since the 1890s, however, night clubs, first in New York City and later in other major cities, had been pioneering a novel style of expressive and participatory entertainment in which drinking played a central role: part of the attraction of the night-club experience no doubt stemmed from the

Jack S. Blocker, Jr. *Alcohol: A Social and Cultural History*, Oxford: Berg, 2006. Copyright © Mack P. Holt 2006. All rights reserved. Reproduced by permission.

"naughty" image given to drinking by the temperance movement. During the new century's first decade, the cultural war over drinking gained greater intensity from the onset of a new, larger wave of immigration, bringing reinforcement to the wet side from the drinking cultures of southern and eastern Europe. Reinforcing this trend, African-Americans, previously among the most abstemious of ethnic groups, adopted urban drinking cultures as they began to migrate in large numbers from the rural South to cities in both North and South. Buoyed both by immigration and by internal migration to the cities, beer consumption continued to rise, and even per capita spirits consumption began to inch upward. During the period 1906–14, per capita consumption of absolute alcohol peaked at about 1.6 US gallons (6.1 liters), about 50 percent higher than the turn-of-the-century level. This upsurge gave added impetus to the dry cause and contributed to the political swing that produced adoption of wartime measures to curb liquor production and then the Eighteenth Amendment, which brought on National Prohibition.

Prohibition Led to Unforeseen Changes

National Prohibition changed drinking in three major ways. First, it seems to have significantly lowered per capita consumption. Obviously, we can never know definitively how much alcohol Americans consumed during Prohibition, and the existing estimates, derived by extrapolation from measures of associated phenomena, depend heavily on their supporting assumptions. The more straightforward estimates show consumption dropping significantly during 1917–18, as the effects of spreading state prohibition laws and federal wartime restrictions on liquor production began to bite. Consumption remained low during the first half of the 1920s, then rebounded somewhat afterward, although still falling short of the pre-Prohibition level. Indices of alcohol-related medical disorders also fell. At the same time, consumption of alternative beverages—milk, coffee, carbonated drinks, and fresh fruit juices—increased. Prohibition therefore wrought a significant change in American drinking habits. The era of diminished consumption was to outlast the end of National Prohibition.

Prohibition altered beverage choices.

Second, Prohibition altered beverage choices. For nearly three-quarters of a century prior to Prohibition, beer had been steadily replacing distilled spirits in American glasses. When the Volstead Act (the Eighteenth Amendment's enforcing law) embargoed all beverages having an alcohol content greater than 0.5 percent, beer was placed at a marked disadvantage relative to spirits because of its lower ratio of cost to weight and higher ratio of price to alcohol content. To a bootlegger, in other words, a choice of spirits made better economic sense. Reversing a historic pattern, hard liquor took the place of beer, contributing about two-thirds of total alcohol consumption by the end of the 1920s. Although winemaking was illegal, production of grape concentrate was not, and California wine-grape growers gleefully discovered a booming market in home vintners.

To present drinking as fashionable was to normalize it.

Finally, the drinking population changed in size and composition, in part reflecting the shift in beverage availability. Beer was the preeminent working-class beverage, and the closing of the saloons and the shortage of beer left many working-class drinkers high and dry. Meanwhile, rebellious youth—mainly middle-class students in colleges and universities—began to use alcohol as a badge of modern, cosmopolitan tastes. Their models were found in the writings of the "Lost Generation" of American intellectuals and on the movie screens of the 1920s; both media portrayed drinking in a radically different light than their pre–World War I counterparts. To present drinking as fashionable was to normalize it, to free it from the negative associations affixed by a century of temperance rhetoric—and at the same time to draw on those associations and that rhetoric for the flavor of cultural rebellion.

Of National Prohibition's three achievements, one—the shift from beer to hard liquor—was destined to be short-lived. The other two, however—the reduction in consumption and the normalization of drinking among middle-class youth— outlasted Prohibition and thus made the 1920s a watershed in the history of American drinking. Because middle-class acceptance of drinking showed greater staying power than Prohibition's induced sobriety, the conventional view of the Prohibition era has emphasized the former while forgetting the latter.

Alcoholism Becomes a Disease

After repeal of the Eighteenth Amendment in 1933, the work of the movies in normalizing drinking was enthusiastically reinforced by the revived liquor industry. "In the post-Prohibition era, advertisers used images of glamour, wealth, and sophistication to promote public drinking and those of domesticity and companionate marriage to encourage household consumption." Women became a prime target for liquor advertising, since they represented the industry's largest untapped market. But other players than drink executives and Hollywood screenwriters also contributed to changing perceptions of drinking. Prohibition had killed the inebriate asylums which had previously provided the institutional foundation for alcohol research; after repeal, a new set of scientists emerged to take the lead in alcohol studies. Their institutional base was Yale University, in particular its Center of Alcohol Studies, and its principal spokesman was a scientist of considerable ability though uncertain credentials, E. M. Jellinek (1890–1963). Jellinek developed and publicized a new view of habitual drunkenness whose central claim was that "alcoholism is a disease." The principal aim of those who formulated the disease concept of alcoholism was to support therapy rather than censure for "alcoholics." The disease concept implicitly opened the door to moderate drinking in the population at large. Howard Haggard, Jellinek's sponsor at Yale, hoped that habits of moderation would prevent drinkers from falling into excess. Basic to the disease concept was the belief that alcoholics suffered from a physiological disorder that rendered their drinking pathological; it followed that those who were not thus afflicted could drink safely, without risking descent into alcoholism. Other scientists independently furnished supportive conclusions. Biologist Frank B. Hanson closed down the long-flourishing line of research into the effects of alcohol on reproduction by claiming persuasively that animal experimentation revealed no genetic consequences whatsoever. Physiologist Yandell Henderson taught Americans to perceive alcohol in the same light as toxic chemicals, namely, as a substance that "could, like [carbon] monoxide, be managed in such a way as to be innocuous." Since alcohol's role in various disorders was supported only by epidemiological rather than clinical evidence, medical scientists in general downplayed its effects.

Home consumption was facilitated further with the arrival of the aluminum beer can in 1934 and the spread of home refrigerators during the 1930s.

Scientific arguments converged neatly with the thrust of a new approach to the treatment of alcoholism. Founded in 1935, by the early 1940s Alcoholics Anonymous (AA) was spreading across the United States. AA played a key role in promulgating the disease concept of alcoholism, adding to scientific claims what appeared to be convincing evidence for the therapeutic value of a treatment strategy premised upon it.

Further support came from the National Council on Alcoholism, an advocacy group devoted to spreading the new gospel.

Drinking Invades the Home

Governments also played a crucial part in normalizing drinking as well as in directing it into particular channels. Immediately following repeal, the federal government played a key regulatory role through the New Deal's National Recovery Administration (NRA), but after the Supreme Court struck down the NRA in 1935, state governments took over primary responsibility for regulation. Those that abandoned their state prohibition statutes generally created their own liquor-control agencies, which preempted the return of licensing into local hands. Licensing regimes were structured to favor off-premise sales, and many states, while establishing government monopolies over spirits sales, now permitted grocery stores to sell beer and, by the 1960s, wine as well. Home consumption was facilitated further with the arrival of the aluminum beer can in 1934 and the spread of home refrigerators during the 1930s. The new regulatory regime aimed to prevent both the return of the saloon and continuation of the lawlessness and disorder that were perceived to have accompanied Prohibition. In a return to the spirit of the colonial period, laws governing alcohol sale and consumption sought to produce social order rather than to foster public health. As a result, drinking returned to the home and surfaced publicly in the new cocktail lounge, in both of which women's drinking was more acceptable than in the old-time saloon.

By the late 1940s, writes cultural historian Lori Rotskoff:

Americans generally viewed drinking as a matter of individual choice and alcoholism as a matter of individual or familial concern. ... [T]he ideological distinction between moderation and alcoholism allowed for the further domestication of drink in the postwar period. By the late 1940s and 1950s, cocktail rituals were woven into the fabric of the

15

dominant culture, both absorbing and reflecting anxieties that accompanied such trends as consumerism, status seeking, social conformity, and the bureaucratization of the corporate workplace.

Advertising Normalizes Drinking

The main contours of the post-repeal world were profoundly shaped by the historical experience of Prohibition and the century of temperance agitation which preceded it. The liquor industry's fervent efforts to make drinking an integral part of everyday life stemmed of course from fear of Prohibition's return. Jellinek and his co-workers explicitly distanced their "scientific" approach from the "moralism" of the temperance movement. State liquor-control agencies were intended to remove the liquor issue from local communities, where it had troubled the waters for more than a century, and thus to depoliticize what had recently furnished the nation's most divisive political issue. The alcohol-control regimes they created sought to prevent at all costs the return of the saloon.

Drinking . . . began to shift from an occasional, often public, act to one that was incorporated into daily life in the home as a marker and accompaniment of leisure.

Prohibition also shaped another major aspect of American drinking during the quarter-century that followed repeal: diminished consumption compared to the immediate pre-Prohibition years. Hard times during the Depression kept consumption low, and the federal government's encouragement of the liquor industry (compared to World War I) helped to boost consumption somewhat during [the] World War II years. But despite the unprecedented prosperity of the late 1940s and 1950s, and despite the normalization of drinking that was occurring since repeal—despite the arrival of the cocktail hour—per capita consumption stubbornly refused to rise significantly until the 1960s. During the entire period from repeal to the election of John F. Kennedy to the presidency, about two-fifths of the adult population reported themselves to be abstainers.

Boomers Change Drinking Attitudes

The drinking scene changed as the baby-boom generation began to reach the older teenage years. Compared to 1960 levels, spirits consumption per capita rose during the ensuing years by about 30 percent, beer by 40 percent, and wine by 75 percent. These significant changes do not, however, seem to have been caused by major alterations in drinking behavior. Survey data show no noteworthy growth in the proportion of drinkers in the male population and only a slight increase in the percentage of women who drank. The key change seems to have been a modification in drinking habits, and one that took place in other Western societies than the United States. Fewer men and women drank only once a month, and more reported drinking daily. Heavy drinking occasions were infrequent, however, and apart from these the amounts consumed were moderate. Drinking, that is, began to shift from an occasional, often public, act to one that was incorporated into daily life in the home as a marker and accompaniment of leisure. Such small alterations in lifestyle were facilitated by the affluence of the period and amplified by the impact of the baby-boom generation, among whose members the changes occurred most notably.

Drinking's upward climb, however, barely outlasted the 1970s. Per capita spirits consumption peaked in 1969 and by 2000 had fallen by more than 40 percent. Beer and wine consumption peaked in 1981 and 1986, respectively, and fell by 12 and 20 percent by 2000. This period of sobering-up is attributed to a spreading health consciousness, aided by concern about drunken driving that led to legislation mandating placement of warning labels on drink containers. Medical scientists' discovery of fetal alcohol syndrome in 1973 may also have helped. Those involved in institutions for treatment of alcoholics, which had blossomed with growing acceptance of the disease concept of alcoholism, by the late 1970s began to engage in an effort to raise societal consciousness about problems caused by drinking. Such concerns received further impetus from the spread of a new self-help therapeutic movement directed at the grown children of drinkers, which took institutional form as the Adult Children of Alcoholics.

Brewing Beer Becomes a Family Activity

As the baby-boom generation aged, at least some of its members became somewhat more selective about what they drank. The background to this recent development is the massive concentration that occurred in the liquor industry during the period since repeal. By the end of the 1930s, four corporations dominated the distilling industry, and these four produced more than three-quarters of the liquor distilled in the USA. In 1935, there were more than 700 brewing companies operating; by 1979 their number had dropped to 45, and by 1984 the four largest firms held a market share of 94 percent. By 1972, led by the vertically integrated Ernest and Julio Gallo Winery, the four largest wineries controlled 53 percent of US wine and brandy shipments. Following the lead of other industries, the liquor industry since the late nineteenth century embraced mass production. Beer was not only brewed in larger batches in massive new breweries, but the brewing process was also accelerated. For the wines and beers that together contributed 70 percent of the alcohol they consumed, some American drinkers increasingly turned to imports and to microbreweries and brewpubs. In 2000, there were more than 1,000 brewpubs and 3,000 microbrew labels in the US. Although microbreweries controlled only 2 percent of the beer market, their segment is a lucrative one, and their growing popularity caused major brewers to diversify their offerings. Another sign of discontent with bland, indistinguishable beer is a rise in home brewing, enabled by federal legislation in 1979. Like drinking at home, where two-thirds of consumption takes place, home brewing closes a circle first inscribed in the early years of American history.

2

Alcohol Use by Underage Youth Is Detrimental

National Household Survey on Drug Abuse

The Substance Abuse and Mental Health Services Administration (SAMHSA) is focused on building resilience and facilitating recovery for people with or at risk for mental or substance use disorders. It periodically publishes the National Household Survey on Drug Use and Health Report, formerly the National Household Survey on Drug Abuse.

Adolescence and young adulthood are critical ages for forming habits and entering social life. Many youth experiment with unlawful drinking—often to disastrous effects. Excessive alcohol use at this age can cause injury, death, vandalism, and can lead to sexual assault. Nearly 3 million underage drinkers meet the criteria for alcohol dependence or alcohol abuse, but not enough receive treatment.

Adolescence and young adulthood are times of transition both physically and socially, and many youthful behaviors can have far-reaching consequences. During this time of social and developmental change, many young people also experiment with alcohol, although all States have had a legal drinking age of 21 since 1988. Regular, excessive alcohol use in adolescence can result in changes in brain functioning and cognitive impairment. Underage drinkers who drive after drinking are at greater risk of fatal crashes than older drinkers

National Household Survey on Drug Abuse, *Alcohol Use by Persons Under the Legal Drinking Age of 21*, Substance Abuse and Mental Health Services Administration (SAMHSA), May 9 2003. www.oas.samhsa.gov/2k3/UnderageDrinking/UnderageDrinking.htm.

because of their lack of driving experience and overconfidence. Among college students, about one fourth reported academic problems related to their alcohol use, and excessive alcohol use can result in death or injury, sexual assault or engaging in unprotected sex, and vandalism or property damage. These problems affect more than just those who engage in underage alcohol use and include risks to other drivers and passengers caused by underage drinking drivers.

Underage alcohol use is more prevalent among males than among females.

National Estimates and Patterns of Underage Alcohol Use

In 2001, 10.1 million people, or 28.5 percent, of persons aged 12 to 20 reported using alcohol in the past month. Nearly one in five persons aged 12 to 20 (19.0 percent, or 6.8 million people) engaged in binge alcohol use in the past month in 2001. Binge alcohol use is defined as having five or more drinks on the same occasion (i.e., at the same time or within a couple of hours) at least once in the past month. Thus, nearly 70 percent of underage persons who drank any alcohol in the past month had at least one occasion in that period when they consumed five or more drinks.

Underage alcohol use is more prevalent among males than among females. An estimated 29.8 percent of males and 27.2 percent of females aged 12 to 20 in 2001 used alcohol in the past month. Rates of binge alcohol use in the past month were 22.0 percent for males aged 12 to 20 and 15.9 percent for females in this age group.

Among racial/ethnic groups, non-Hispanic whites in the 12 to 20 age group had the highest rate of past month alcohol use (31.6 percent). Non-Hispanic blacks and Asians in this age group had the lowest rates (19.8 and 19.7 percent, respectively). Similar patterns were observed for binge alcohol use by Hispanic origin and race.

Rates of past month alcohol use by county type for persons aged 12 to 20 were 27.3 percent for persons living in large metropolitan areas, 29.8 percent for those in small metropolitan areas, and 29.3 percent for those in nonmetropolitan areas. For binge alcohol use in the past month by county type, rates ranged from 17.7 percent in large metropolitan areas to 21.0 percent in nonmetropolitan areas.

Rates of any alcohol use in the past month for specific ages increased up to age 21 (67.5 percent), the legal drinking age, and remained above 60 percent through age 25. Rates roughly doubled from age 12 (2.6 percent) to age 13 (6.1 percent), from age 13 to age 14 (11.7 percent), and from age 14 to age 15 (21.5 percent). In addition, more than half of young adults aged 19 or 20 and nearly 45 percent of 18 year olds had used alcohol in the past month.

Rates of binge alcohol use in the past month for specific ages showed a pattern of steady increases similar to that for any alcohol use, peaking at age 21. Nearly half of 21 year olds (48.2 percent) engaged in binge alcohol use at some point in the past month. In addition, nearly 40 percent of young adults aged 19 or 20 were binge alcohol users in 2001. Approximately one in eight 15 year olds, 18 percent of 16 year olds, and nearly one fourth of 17 year olds were binge alcohol users in the past month.

Full-time undergraduates aged 18 to 20 were significantly more likely to have used alcohol in the past month or to have engaged in binge alcohol use in the past month compared with their counterparts who were not in college full time.

State Estimates of Underage Alcohol Use

Underage alcohol use in the past month at the State level ranged from a low of 16.1 percent of persons aged 12 to 20 in

Utah to 39.6 percent of this age group in North Dakota. Underage alcohol use tended to be more prevalent in States in New England, the upper Midwest, and the northern Mountain States of Montana and Wyoming. Six of the ten States with the lowest rates of underage alcohol use were located in the Southeast. In addition to Utah in the West, Idaho had one of the lowest rates of underage alcohol use (22.8 percent). Although Southeastern States tended to have lower rates of underage alcohol use, Louisiana was an exception, with an estimated 32.5 percent of persons aged 12 to 20 having used alcohol in the past month.

Problems Associated with Underage Alcohol Use

Two important issues of concern related to underage alcohol use are motor vehicle accidents resulting from driving under the influence of alcohol and the need for treatment for alcohol use disorders among youth. . . . Estimates in this section are based on the 2001 NHSDA [National Household Survey on Drug Abuse].

In 2001, nearly 3 million persons aged 16 to 20 were estimated to have driven under the influence of alcohol at least once in the past year, including more than 600,000 persons aged 16 or 17.

In 2001, nearly 3 million persons aged 16 to 20 were estimated to have driven under the influence of alcohol at least once in the past year, including more than 600,000 persons aged 16 or 17. The rate of driving under the influence of alcohol in the past year for 16 to 25 year olds peaked at age 21 (28.3 percent) and then declined for ages 22 to 25.

Nearly 3 million persons aged 12 to 20 were classified as meeting criteria for alcohol dependence or abuse in the past 12 months, based on the numbers of alcohol-related problems they experienced in that period. In comparison, however, only about 400,000 persons in this age group were estimated to have received any type of alcohol treatment in the past year. This latter finding suggests considerable unmet need for alcohol treatment among underage drinkers experiencing problems related to their alcohol use.

3

The Legal Drinking Age Is Outdated and Should Be Lowered

John J. Miller

John J. Miller is a political reporter for the conservative publication National Review.

Many politicians and lobbyists find the legal drinking age of twenty-one to be a great success, praising it for reducing drunk driving fatalities without considering that other factors, such as seat belt laws and safer cars, have helped. The U.S. government sends soldiers under the age of twenty-one off to war, where they might have to kill or be killed, and yet prohibits them from having a beer. Instead of driving young adults into unlawful and possibly dangerous situations by drinking illegally, the law should be changed to lower the drinking age.

In the first four years of Operation Iraqi Freedom, 563 Americans under the age of 21 were killed in the line of duty. These citizen soldiers were old enough to vote, old enough to put on military uniforms, and old enough to die for their country: They were old enough to do just about anything, except drink a red-white-and-blue can of Budweiser.

Apparently they weren't grown-up enough to enjoy that privilege.

That's because when it comes to alcohol, the United States is more like Indonesia, Mongolia, and Palau than the rest of

John J. Miller, "The Case Against 21," *National Review Online*, April 19, 2007. Reproduced by permission.

the world: It is one of just four countries that requires people to be at least 21 years old to buy booze. *The only countries with stiffer [drinking] laws are Islamic ones.*

Many public-health advocates regard this latter-day prohibition as a great triumph. Mothers Against Drunk Driving [MADD] says on its website that setting the legal drinking age at 21, rather than 18, has saved "more than 21,000 lives" from alcohol-related traffic fatalities.

It certainly sounds like a success story. But is it really so simple?

Looking at the Larger Picture

The former president of Middlebury College says that the picture is in fact far more complicated.

"It's just not true," says John M. McCardell Jr. of MADD's assertion. "I'm not going to claim that legal-age 21 has saved no lives at all, but it's just one factor among many and it's not anywhere near the most important factor."

McCardell is the head of Choose Responsibility, a new nonprofit group that calls for lowering the drinking age. He is also the primary author of a draft report on the 21-year-old drinking age.

Three years ago, after stepping down as the head of Middlebury, McCardell penned an op-ed for the *New York Times* called "What Your College President Didn't Tell You." He criticized tenure and argued that low student-faculty ratios are overrated. He also said that the 21-year-old drinking age "is bad social policy and terrible law."

This last idea sparked the interest of the Robertson Foundation, which encouraged McCardell to write the 224-page paper that Choose Responsibility is now circulating among academics and other interested parties. Although McCardell describes the paper as a "work in progress," it is in fact a devastating critique of the 21-year-old drinking age. . . .

What annoys McCardell most is the recurring claim that the raised drinking age has saved more than 21,000 lives. "That's talking point [number] 1 for modern temperance organizations, but they can't point to any data that show a cause and effect," he says.

As his report reveals, alcohol-related driving fatalities have fallen sharply since 1982, when a presidential commission on drunk driving urged states to raise their drinking ages to 21. That year, there were 1.64 deaths per 100 million vehicle miles of travel; in 2001, there were 0.63 deaths. That's a drop of 62 percent.

Seatbelts Have Made a Difference

This is an important achievement. Yet the drinking age probably played only a small role. The dramatic increase in seatbelt use almost certainly accounts for most of the improvement. The National Highway Transportation Safety Administration says that the proper use of seatbelts reduces the odds of death for front-seat passengers involved in car crashes by 45 percent. In 1984, when President [Ronald] Reagan linked federal highway funds to the 21-year drinking age, about 14 percent of motorists used seatbelts. By 2004, this figure had shot up to 80 percent. Also during this period, life-saving air bags became a standard feature on cars.

As a society, we've become a lot more aware of the problem of drunk driving.

What's more, alcohol-related fatalities were beginning to decline before the movement for a raised drinking age got off the ground, thanks to a cultural shift. "*As a society, we've become a lot more aware of the problem of drunk driving*," says McCardell. "When I was in school, nobody used the term 'designated driver.'" Demographic forces helped out, too: In the 1980s, following the Baby Boom [the post–World War II era until 1964 when U.S. *births* rose dramatically], the population of young people actually shrank. Fewer young drivers means fewer high-risk drivers, and so even if attitudes about seatbelts and drunk driving hadn't changed, there almost certainly would have been a reduction in traffic deaths anyway.

McCardell suggests that one effect of raising the drinking age was not to prevent deaths but merely to delay them. "The most common age for drinking-related deaths is now 21, followed by 22 and 23," he says. "It seems that the minimum drinking age is as likely to have postponed fatalities as to have reduced them."

There's even a case to be made that the higher drinking age has had negative consequences. It encourages disrespect for the law. It usurps the role of parents in teaching their children about the proper use of alcohol, especially in the many states where it's illegal for them even to let their 18-year-old children have a glass of wine at a Thanksgiving dinner.

"There used to be an intergenerational social intercourse that's now completely gone—the law obliterated it," says Mc-Cardell. "If you expect adult behavior, you're more likely to get it than if you infantilize people." Is it a coincidence that one of the most commonly cited campus problems is binge drinking?

The Benefits of the Minimum Legal Drinking Age Are a Myth

Despite this, the mythology about the drinking age persists in popular culture and in politics. Three years ago, when Pete Coors [chairman of Coors Brewing Co.] ran for the Senate in Colorado, his opponent's campaign dredged up an interview Coors had given to *USA Today* in 1997. "Maybe the answer is lowering the drinking age so that kids learn to be responsible about drinking at a younger age," said Coors. "I'm not an advocate of trying to get people to drink, but kids are drinking now anyway. All we've done is criminalize them." (He also called for "zero tolerance" for drinking and driving and other alcohol-related crimes, but this was not widely reported.)

Thus was born a mini-scandal over Coors and his candidacy. Was the scion of a famous beer family running for the Senate so he could change the law and expand his customer base? Suddenly and unexpectedly, the drinking age became an issue in the race. "Now it pops up nearly everywhere Coors goes," reported the *Denver Post*. Coors's opponent, Ken Salazar, leaned heavily on those bogus MADD numbers: "What would end up happening [if the federal government lowered the drinking age] is we'd end up losing as many as 1,000 young people's lives each year." Salazar went on to defeat Coors for several reasons—he was already a popular public official, it was a good year to run as a Democrat in Colorado, and so on—and one of them was this controversy.

An unpopular idea is not necessarily a bad idea, however. McCardell's research makes a strong case against the federally mandated drinking age. Choose Responsibility, which receives no financial support from the beer, wine, or liquor companies, is committed to making sure that we hear it.

I'm convinced: The time has come to lower the drinking age to 18, or perhaps to let states experiment with lowering it. At the very least, shouldn't soldiers who are trusted with M-16s [military rifles] also be trusted with six packs?

4

Arguments for Lowering the Legal Drinking Age Are Not Valid

AlcoholPolicyMD.com

Many arguments in favor of lowering the legal minimum drinking age of twenty-one are misleading or false. Opponents argue that alcohol should not be a forbidden fruit and that drinking responsibly can be taught. Yet overwhelming evidence suggests that by lowering the drinking age, alcohol abuse among teenagers and preteens would start even earlier than it does now. Also nobody has a viable plan for teaching adolescents to drink without endangering their own or others' lives. The legal drinking age has saved many lives and lowering it would only exacerbate the drinking problem.

Enforcement of age-21 laws has multiple ramifications in college settings, where underage students, often a majority on campus, co-mingle with students of legal age. College administrators face serious questions about how and whether to enforce the minimum legal drinking age (MLDA). They must balance safety, liability, and law-enforcement responsibilities with universities' historic role as havens of personal freedom, experimentation, and student self-expression and individual responsibility. Administrators' responses become all the more difficult because most students begin drinking well before they arrive on campus.

"Addressing the Minimum Legal Drinking Age (MLDA) in College Communities," *AlcoholPolicyMD.com*, 2005. © 2005 Alcoholpolicymd.com. All rights reserved. Reproduced by permission. www.alcoholpolicymd.com/alcohol_and_health/study_legal_age.htm.

Not surprisingly, many administrators focus more on binge or high-risk drinking by their students and the host of problems it creates. The age of the drinker often becomes a secondary concern as campus alcohol policies also emphasize "harm reduction" over prevention. Enforcement of the MLDA has historically focused heavily on individual education and punishment of violators. Colleges are now learning that effective action on the MLDA requires a broader prevention approach that affects the conditions under which alcohol is made available, promoted and integrated into college life. Conversely, universities have found that the MLDA provides a strong legal rationale to develop effective prevention policies that can reduce high-risk as well as underage drinking.

If 18 year-olds get the OK to drink, they will be modeling drinking for younger teens.

The History of the MLDA

Following the repeal of Prohibition [the law banning alcohol consumption, purchase, and sale] in 1933, many states set the MLDA at 21 (and in some cases 18 for the purchase of beer). During the 1960s and 1970s, many states lowered the MLDA in response to growing political liberalism and Vietnam war-era arguments that the drinking age should parallel the draft age of 18. Subsequently:

> In 1982, prompted by evidence linking younger drinking ages with increased alcohol-related highway deaths among youths, President Ronald Reagan appointed a Presidential Commission on Drunk Driving. Its top recommendation was the passage of federal legislation to require all states to raise the MLDA to 21.

> In 1984, 23 states had minimum alcohol purchasing ages of 21 years old, and on July 17th of that year, President Ronald Reagan signed legislation to withhold federal highway funds from the remaining 27 states if they did not follow suit.

The age-21 MLDA was universally adopted nationwide as of July 1, 1998, when Wyoming became the last state to raise its drinking age to 21. . . .

Answering MLDA Critics

Despite the MLDA's impressive public health successes, opponents level several common arguments against it. These arguments often spring from alcoholic-beverage industry sources or their paid industry-funded representatives, including substance abuse researchers. Common arguments that attack MLDA laws and policies (and responses to them) include:

No education program has successfully taught entire populations of youth to drink responsibly.

The "Forbidden Fruit" Argument

Some have argued that lowering the drinking age will reduce the allure of alcohol as a "forbidden fruit" for minors. In fact, research suggests that lowering the drinking age will make alcohol more available to an even younger population, replacing "forbidden fruit" with "low-hanging fruit." The practices and behaviors of 18 year-olds are particularly influential on 15 to 17 year-olds. If 18 year-olds get the OK to drink, they will be modeling drinking for younger teens. Legal access to alcohol for 18 year-olds will provide more opportunities for younger teens to obtain it illegally from older peers, making enforcement that much more difficult among high school students. For this reason, parents and schools strongly supported the age-21 MLDA.

Despite the call by some university administrators to lower the drinking age (thus relieving them of enforcement responsibilities), there is no evidence that there were fewer campus alcohol problems when lower drinking ages were in effect. In fact, age-21 has resulted in decreases, not increases, in youth drinking, an outcome inconsistent with an increased allure of alcohol. In 1983, one year before the National Minimum Purchase Age Act was passed, 88% of high school seniors reported any alcohol use in the past year and 41% reported binge drinking. By 2000, alcohol use by seniors had dropped to 73% and the percentage of binge drinkers had fallen to 30%.

The "Teach Responsible Drinking" Argument

Critics have argued that lowering the drinking age will encourage young people to be responsible consumers. They'll get an idea of their tolerance and learn to drink under supervision at bars (or on campus, if in college), rather than at uncontrolled private parties away from school. However, there is no evidence to indicate that kids will learn to drink responsibly simply because they are able to consume alcohol legally at a younger age. Countries with lower drinking ages suffer from alcohol-related problems similar to those in the U.S. It was recently reported that New Zealand is considering raising its drinking age to 21 again after rates of teen binge drinking and drunken fighting increased when that country lowered its drinking age to 18 in 1999.

Research documents some promising results for one-on-one interventions with individual problem drinkers to help them moderate their consumption. However, no education program has successfully taught entire populations of youth to drink responsibly. Responsible consumption comes with maturity, and maturity largely comes as certain protective mechanisms, such as marriage and a first job, begin to take hold. Providing supervision does not necessarily lead to responsibility. For example, some campuses have student pubs that practice responsible beverage service and cater also to faculty who ostensibly model responsible drinking. No evidence that the presence of such facilities reduces high-risk student drinking in other venues on and around campus.

Many bars, on the other hand, aggressively promote irresponsible drinking by deeply discounting drinks and by heavily promoting specials, such as happy hours, two-for-ones, all-you-can-drink nights, and bar crawls.

Age-21 laws help keep young people healthy by postponing the onset of alcohol use.

Age of Initiation Argument

Another common argument holds that at age 18, kids can vote, join the military, sign contracts, and even smoke. Why shouldn't they be able to drink? Ages of initiation indeed vary—one may vote at 18, drink at 21, rent a car at 25, and run for president at 35. These ages may appear arbitrary, but they take into account the requirements, risks, and benefits of each act.

When age-21 was challenged in Louisiana's State Supreme Court, the Court upheld the law, ruling that ". . . statutes establishing the minimum drinking age at a higher level than the age of majority are not arbitrary because they substantially further the appropriate governmental purpose of improving highway safety, and thus are constitutional."

Age-21 laws held keep young people healthy by postponing the onset of alcohol use. Deferred drinking reduces the risks of:

- developing alcohol dependence or abuse later in life

- harming the developing brain, a developmental process that continues into the early 20's

- engaging in current and adult drug use

- suffering alcohol-related problems, such as trouble at work, with friends, family, and police

Defeatist Argument: "Minors Still Drink, so Age-21 Laws Clearly Don't Work."

Age-21 laws work. Young people drink less in response. The laws have saved an estimated 20,043 lives since states began implementing them in 1975, and they've decreased the number of alcohol-related youth fatalities among drivers by 63% since 1982.

> Stricter enforcement of age-21 laws against commercial sellers would make those laws even more effective at reducing youth access to alcohol. The ease with which young people acquire alcohol—nearly three-quarters of 8th graders (71%) say that it is "fairly easy" or "very easy" to get—indicates that more must be done. Current laws against sales to minors need stiff penalties to deter violations. Better education and prevention-oriented laws are needed to reduce the commercial pressures on kids to drink.

Finally, the most compelling need for age 21 is the clear evidence that lowering the drinking age in the past has sacrificed public health and safety:

- State motor vehicle fatality data from the 48 continental states found that lowering the drinking age for beer from 21 to 18 resulted in an 11% increase in fatalities among that age group.

- In Arizona, lowering the drinking age increased the incidence of fatal accidents by more than 25% and traffic fatalities by more than 35%.

- Lowering the drinking age in Massachusetts caused an increase in total fatal crashes, alcohol-related fatal crashes, and alcohol-related property damage crashes among 18 to 20 year-old drivers.

- From 1979 to 1984, the suicide rate was 9.7% greater among young people who could legally drink alcohol than among their peers who could not.

Despite occasional challenges and the certainty that it is neither universally enforced or observed, the MLDA continues to enjoy strong public support among both adults and teens. An Associated Press poll conducted in June 2001 found that

68% of teens and adults supported keeping the drinking age at 21, while 16% of teens and 15% of adults supported raising it.

5

The Legal Drinking Age Exacerbates Underage Drinking

Dennis Tamburello

Dennis Tamburello is a Franciscan friar and a professor of religious studies at Siena College, in Loudonville, New York.

The legal drinking age of twenty-one, far from being the solution to the problem of underage drinking, has forced young adults eighteen to twenty to drink illegally and without supervision. Instead of saving lives, it endangers lives, because adolescents have no chance of learning how to drink responsibly. Yet the legal drinking age cannot be lowered without a change in our culture, along with more responsible and mature behavior by teenagers. Only then can we hope to lessen the dangers of drinking and drunk driving.

Everyone knows that excessive drinking poses many dangers, including the risk of car accidents, injuries, and fights. But according to the latest research, there are additional risks for adolescents. Alcohol significantly impairs overall brain functions in the young, particularly cognitive functions like memory, learning, spatial skills, and decision-making skills—and these impairments get worse as heavy drinking continues. Author Katy Butler states [in a 2006 *New York Times* article]:

> Mounting research suggests that alcohol causes more damage to the developing brains of teenagers than was previously thought, injuring them significantly more than it does

Friar Dennis Tamburello, "Clean and Sober," *Timesunion.com*, July 15, 2006. Reproduced by permission. http://blogs.timesunion.com/tamburello/?p=12.

adult brains. The findings, though preliminary, have demolished the assumption that people can drink heavily for years before causing themselves significant neurological injury. And the research even suggests that early heavy drinking may undermine the precise neurological capacities needed to protect oneself from alcoholism.

Tell me something I don't know.

In over twenty years of college teaching—and living among students in the residence halls—I have observed more than my share of excessive drinking. It's not that all students are drinking; in fact, a sizable percentage of students drink very little or not at all, a fact that I delight in pointing out to students who excuse their heavy drinking with the mantra, "Everyone is doing it. It's part of being in college."

For several years, I taught an alcohol-awareness course that was crafted by the Prevention Research Institute. Since then I have been intensely interested in the ongoing research in this field. One recent article affirmed what I had long suspected and feared: statistics show that the amount of "binge" drinking among college-age students *is* on the rise. (I should note that there seems to be some disagreement among researchers on what constitutes binge drinking, so not everyone agrees with that last statement. But everyone agrees that binge drinking, whatever its extent, is a problem in our society.)

I remain convinced that a person who is old enough to die for his/her country is old enough to have a few (note the adjective) drinks.

There Are No Easy Solutions

It's hard to know what is the best way to get the message to sink in to students about the dangers of alcohol abuse. Simply giving students the necessary information doesn't seem to work for most of the high-risk drinkers. They *know* they should not drink the way they do, but they don't have the *will* to stop. The training from Prevention Research Institute helped me to understand how psychological dependency on alcohol generally precedes physical dependency.

At this point in my life, I have come to the following conclusions about adolescents and drinking:

- The raising of the legal drinking age to 21 is part of the problem, not the solution. Many have argued that raising the drinking age has led to fewer traffic fatalities among people under 21. However, I have seen no solid evidence that the legal drinking age of 21 is the *direct cause* of the decrease in these fatalities. (Correlation is not the same thing as causality.) In fact, there is evidence that alcohol-related traffic fatalities have *increased for people aged 21 to 24* since the legal drinking age was changed. A more likely reason for the decrease in fatalities in the under-21 age group is the increased use of designated drivers.

- I remain convinced that a person who is old enough to die for his/her country is old enough to have a few (note the adjective) drinks. At age 18, a person is old enough to vote, get married, sign legal contracts, and do many other adult things. At the same time, we should insist that if people want to be treated like adults, they must *act* like adults. This is difficult in a society where adolescence sometimes extends into people's thirties.

- Prohibition didn't work in the past, and it's not working now. My experience in working with college students has convinced me that making alcohol a "forbidden fruit" is counterproductive. (This strategy has failed since the time of Adam and Eve.) It would be better to allow it, while creating a culture in which it is socially unacceptable to abuse it.

- This means that we "older" folks need to take a look at what messages we send to youth by our own drinking habits. In my opinion, many sectors of our society have an unhealthy approach to alcohol. We need to discourage overconsumption of alcoholic beverages at any age. Everybody knows that consuming small amounts of alcohol can actually be beneficial to health, like the glass of wine many people have with dinner. On the other hand, much research shows that more than a few drinks per day can lead to all kinds of health problems. We now know that this is especially true for people under 20.

Teenagers Who Drink Excessively Risk Severe Dangers

In the words of a recovering drug addict whom I once met, when you abuse your body with alcohol and/or drugs, "sooner or later you will have to pay the piper." She was referring to health problems that emerged many years after she was clean and sober. Most teens don't want to think about how their youthful excesses will come back to bite them in the butt later in life. But some of those bad effects show up right away. I often wonder if the lack of motivation and poor performance of some of my students is not directly related to drinking—to say nothing of the problems of serious injuries, sexual assault, and blackouts.

Changing the culture of drinking on college campuses, and in society as a whole, will take a lot of work. In my experience, drinking in Europe tends to be more of an accompaniment to a good meal or a social event, rather than an end in itself. (This is not to say that Europe doesn't have its share of people with alcoholism.) Excessive drinking is frowned upon, and drunk driving is rewarded with draconian penalties. These are the kinds of attitudes and policies I'd like to see more in the U.S.

I want to make it clear to my younger readers that I do not advocate breaking the law. At the same time, we as a society need to look at the current legal drinking age in most of the states, and honestly ask whether it has helped the situation. In my opinion, it has been a failed experiment. But lowering the legal drinking age will not in itself resolve the problem, unless it is accompanied by a major change in attitudes and behaviors. Teens don't want to hear this, but to a great extent, they brought the higher legal drinking age upon themselves by their age group's irresponsible conduct.

Abusing the Body Is Immoral

Most branches of Christianity do not forbid all drinking. After all, Jesus himself was known to drink wine. But our scriptures do insist on the importance of taking care of ourselves and others. In his first letter to the Corinthians, St. Paul says, "Do you not know that your body is a temple of the holy Spirit within you, whom you have from God, and you are not your own?" Contrary to how many Christians have interpreted Paul, he does not think the body is evil; but the *abuse* of our body (or anyone else's, for that matter) is.

I sincerely hope that our young people will take the latest research on adolescent drinking to heart. It will do good for a lot more than their neurons.

6

A Drinking Permit Should Replace the Minimum Legal Drinking Age

David J. Hanson, Dwight B. Heath, and Joel S. Rudy

David J. Hanson, is a professor emeritus of sociology at the State University of New York at Potsdam. Dwight B. Heath is a professor of anthropology at Brown University and the author of Drinking Occasions *and* International Handbook on Alcohol and Culture. *Joel S. Rudy is the vice president and dean of students emeritus at Ohio State University.*

Underage drinking is a severe problem on college campuses nationwide, yet age-based prohibition has not led to the expected results. Instead a provisional drinking permit, similar to a learner's permit for driving, can teach young adults how to drink responsibly, and without the fear and the excitement of breaking the law. Outlawing alcohol only leads to binge drinking, whereas a supervised drinking permit will allow teenagers to become responsible drinkers.

In a majority of states in the U.S., drivers aged 16 and 17 gain valuable experience while holding special licenses that restrict the conditions under which they may drive (for example, only in daylight hours, only with a regularly-licensed driver in the car, etc.). This provides a slow and safe introduction to an adult privilege. The same general concept should be adapted to apply to drinking.

David J. Hanson, Dwight B. Heath, and Joel S. Rudy, "What About the Drinking Age?" *Alcohol: Problems and Solutions,* August 12, 2007. Reproduced by permission. www2.potsdam.edu/hansondj/YouthIssues/1046347764.html.

42

An "apparently underage" young woman is holding a drink in an off-campus bar. When the police raid the establishment, she is questioned and cited for underage consumption. The event—with no accidents, deaths or riots—is seemingly unremarkable, but makes national news because the young woman is President [George W.] Bush's daughter. But isn't the news more about who Jenna Bush is than what she has done? Have we not yet become tired of unreasonable underage drinking stories?

Compare this "newsworthy" item to other underage drinking stories. Each college term, we hear accounts of a small group of students who risk acute alcohol poisoning during rituals like "21 for 21"—downing on their 21st birthday a shot of liquor for every year of their life. In dorm rooms and in off-campus apartments, sometimes-depressed students hole up with a bottle of alcohol, start to chug and are lucky if their failed cure brings nothing more than heaves and a headache. Underclassmen find alcohol parties tied to the "Big Game," drink themselves insensible and fall to their death off balconies. It's all been in the newspapers, this waste of promising young lives that shocks us all.

Age-Based Prohibition Is Not the Solution

One predictable reaction to accounts of injuries or death among these "adults"—those old enough to go to war, marry, vote, sign binding contracts, but not buy a single draft beer—has been to further tighten age-based prohibition. And, indeed, it is a growing response to incidence of alcohol consumption by college students.

Policing is stepped up, penalties mount, task forces produce increasingly exotic ideas about how to quarantine young adults (even those who demonstrate the ability to drink moderately and responsibly) from alcohol beverages. Yet amid the countermeasures, the tragedies continue but are now accompanied by "sensational" citations for breaking the law.

Having a bird's eye view of collegiate drinking as both keen observers of drinking and its outcomes and long-term members of campus life, we would like to suggest an alternative to zero tolerance: a system of gradual access to alcohol beverages by consumption-inclined 19- and 20-year-olds. Why not teach responsible drinking behavior under mature supervision, rather than leave these young adults to experiment on their own?

Consider the fallacy of the prohibition that now governs almost every U.S. institution of higher learning. At freshman orientation, half of the students are already "regular" drinkers by some definition. The newcomers immediately become members of a peculiarly narrow community.

Zero Tolerance Only Leads to Rebellion

Almost everyone is within a five-year age bracket. Through fraternities, sororities, other social organizations, dating, and less formal socializing, this narrow age group (18–22) thoroughly intermingles. Yet in any social setting where alcohol is present, the law says those 21 and older may drink beer, wine and distilled spirits in unlimited quantities as long as they do not drive or appear intoxicated in public; those age 20 years, 364 days or younger must stick with soft drinks or become lawbreakers.

The modern age-based prohibition seems to be working no better than the 1920s version; while a smaller percentage of young adults are now drinking, a sizable minority is drinking recklessly.

Should anyone be surprised that zero tolerance is met with rebellion and rule breaking? Outlandish behavior is a typical reaction to prohibition, which is why the illegal speakeasies were always bawdier than the public bars that the Volstead Act [National Prohibition Act of 1919] shut down. The modern age-based prohibition seems to be working no better than the 1920s version; while a smaller percentage of young adults are now drinking, a sizable minority is drinking recklessly. Is there a ready solution? We offer one for consideration and debate: a provisional drinking license.

In more than 30 states, drivers aged 16 and 17 gain driving experience while holding special licenses that restrict when and how they may drive (for example, no late-night cruising). This permits a slow introduction to an adult privilege. The same concept should apply to drinking.

What could be the elements of a provisional drinking license? There could be time and place restrictions. The license holder could drink, for example, only in an establishment where at least 75% of sales receipts were for food (no bars, no liquor-store purchases). No service after 11:00 pm. Moreover, a 19- or 20-year-old could have to undergo formal instruction about alcohol and pass a licensing exam. Parents and other authorities could unilaterally revoke/suspend the special license without which service/consumption would be illegal. In addition, this provision would not be accompanied by any changes to the current .02% BAC [blood alcohol concentration] law for under-21 drivers.

Drinking Responsibly Can Be Learned

We realize that some few young people would undoubtedly still continue to drink too much, too fast, for the wrong reasons, or in risky settings. But for the Jenna Bush's of the world (by all accounts she was not exhibiting out-of-control drinking behavior) the vast majority who are eager to learn but denied any sensible opportunities, clandestine overindulgence could give way to public self-regulation, with the penalty for abuse being revocation of the privilege. Young people would learn to accept alcohol for what it is, a socially acceptable beverage in need of respect, rather than mythologizing it as a source of magical empowerment that increases with every gulp. Gone, too, would be scenarios that invite contempt for the current law—the inability of two 20-year-olds to drink champagne at their own wedding, for example.

It's time to normalize behaviors at a moderate level rather than to continue to drive them underground to everyone's detriment.

On the campuses or within organizations where we teach and work, we delight in seeing emerging adults grow in academic knowledge and in life-skills, turning before our eyes into competent adults. To leave alcohol outside this process, the record shows, is foolish and dangerous.

It's time to normalize behaviors at a moderate level rather than to continue to drive them underground to everyone's detriment. It is time to teach through trust and potential rather than through blame, accusation and guilt. It is time to open the doors to constructive debate rather than to keep them locked and continue to contribute to the consequences of the forbidden fruit syndrome. Let the discussions begin.

7

Young Adults Should Be Taught Responsible Drinking

Stanton Peele

Stanton Peele is a forensic psychologist and has been writing about addiction since 1969.

Alcohol abuse and especially binge drinking are a real problem in the United States, yet the legal drinking age will never be able to solve it. Instead of outlawing alcohol and forcing teenagers to drink in private and without any parental or other guidance, sensible drinking should be taught and promoted. To reduce the dangers of bingeing, teenagers have to learn how to drink responsibly. If not, they will be driven underground and continue to harm themselves.

Telling underage drinkers they won't have access to alcohol only increases their motivation to drink, whether they are exposed to alcohol cues or not.

This [is] . . . why the American prohibitionist model of alcohol education and control for young people is doomed to fail. To start, keep in mind that the United States is the only Western nation to make drinking illegal until people turn 21. Yet efforts to restrict access to alcohol for youthful drinkers, according to the current study, are only likely to exacerbate their urge to drink.

According to the government's National Survey on Drug Use and Health, "In 2005, about 10.8 million persons aged 12

Stanton Peele, "The Bizarre Effort to Eliminate Underage Drinking in the U.S.: A Harm Reduction Approach to Youthful Drinking," *Addiction Research & Theory*, vol. 15, 2007, p. 227–29. Reproduced by permission.

to 20 (28 percent of this age group) reported drinking alcohol in the past month. And nearly 7.2 million (19 percent of all youths and 70 percent of those who drink) were binge drinkers"—that is, having five or more drinks at least once a month. Beyond this, 2.3 million (6 percent of all youths and 20 percent of youths who drink) were "heavy drinkers" (frequent binge drinkers).

Young Drinkers Need Guidance

These are quite startling figures—but they don't capture the extent and resulting peril of unhealthy drinking by Americans as they approach and then achieve the age of 21, when they can drink legally. More than half of those 18 to 20 had at least one drink in the last month, as have more than two-thirds of those between the ages of 21 and 25.

Young drinkers don't drink well.

Young drinkers don't drink well. More than a third of all young people between 18 and 20 (36 percent) binge drink, as do 46 percent among those aged 21 to 25. Thus bingeing gets even worse when young people can drink legally—at age 21, *half of all Americans binge!* When intoxicated, young Americans do dangerous things—20 percent of 18 to 20 year olds, and 28 percent of 21 to 25 year olds, report having driven under the influence of alcohol in the past year. . . .

Nobody Dares to Touch the Minimum Legal Drinking Age Law

In 2006, the U.S. House of Representatives passed *The Sober Truth on Preventing Underage Drinking (STOP)* by a vote of 373–23, which the Senate then promptly endorsed unanimously. According to Rep. Tom Osborne (R-Neb.), one of the bill's cosponsors, the legislation is necessary because "the Centers for Disease Control and Prevention estimated the number of underage deaths due to excessive alcohol use at 4,554 a year." Whereas 23 senators voted against the resolution that authorized the invasion of Iraq, none dared oppose this jihad. The bill was supported by a wide range of government agencies, alcohol producers and sellers, and public interest groups.

Yet the bill is redundant, since underage drinking is by definition already illegal. The legislation's supporters are not daunted that we have been fighting underage drinking for decades, since the drinking age was raised nationally to 21. Although there is evidence that raising the age limit reduced traffic fatalities, drunk driving has been increasing since the late 1990s among both high school and college students.

Moreover, the offsetting drawbacks of America's singular age restrictions on drinking have not been remedied, as the current legislation once again attempts to do.

The Minimum Legal Drinking Age Law Forces Young People to Drink Privately

One reason every other comparable country permits what Americans consider to be "underage" drinking (including drinking by Americans over 18 who are capable of volunteering to face death fighting in Iraq) is that they want to keep such drinking public, to reduce resulting harms.

If our goal is to eliminate all underage drinking, we certainly have our work cut out for us. As the American data make clear, underage drinking and bingeing is commonplace, and by their late teens, typical of Americans (the U.S. shares this characteristic with many countries, although other countries, primarily around the Mediterranean, have less adolescent bingeing). Striving to eliminate something that has reached this critical mass is quixotic.

And what if we could eliminate such underage drinking? What would happen when all those abstinent youths can suddenly drink legally? Would they drink any better than young adults currently do? After all, how would they have learned to drink moderately and sensibly? A sister study to the U.S. National Survey, the Monitoring the Future survey, finds that more high school seniors disapprove of regular moderate drinking than disapprove of periodic bingeing. Somehow, the alcohol education they receive leads them to prefer bingeing!

Binge Drinking Is the Real Danger

Even recognizing the high levels of underage drinking that will undoubtedly continue to occur, could we nonetheless discourage bingeing? Instead of stressing the elimination of all youthful drinking, we could use education and public service announcements to distinguish "sensible" from excessive and dangerous drinking, including not only safe levels of drinking but taking steps to reduce harms from drunkenness, such as arranging safe rides. . . .

Students can be taught the different consequences of binge drinking and regular moderate drinking.

Students can be taught the different consequences of binge drinking and regular moderate drinking. For instance, the government's *Dietary Guidelines for Americans* recommends 1–2 drinks daily for adult Americans who drink, since this level of consumption is associated with reduced heart disease. Binge drinking, on the other hand, is particularly damaging neurologically to young brains.

Saying that alcohol consumption is inevitably negative—that it leads only to risky behavior and alcoholism—is a temperance message that causes youth to reject all messages about safe drinking, the same way they reject inaccurate messages about illicit drugs such as marijuana.

8

Cultural Exposure to Alcohol Does Not Lead to Responsible Drinking

Coalition for a Safe and Drug-Free Nevada

While many believe that European countries have fewer alcohol-related problems than the United States, evidence shows that this view is inaccurate. Young European adults, on average, do not drink more responsibly that their American counterparts. The argument that a lower drinking age leads to more responsible alcohol consumption is not valid, and there is no evidence that the lower drinking age prevalent in Europe leads to lower levels of alcohol abuse.

There is a commonly held perception that American youth drink more frequently and experience more alcohol-related problems than do their European counterparts. This perception, in turn, is often utilized as argument for various changes in U.S. alcohol policies and prevention initiatives, including elimination of minimum drinking age laws and development of programs that teach "responsible" drinking to youth.

A great majority of the European countries have higher intoxication rates among youth than the United States and less than a quarter had lower rates or equivalent rates to the United States.

Joel Grube, "Youth Drinking Rates and Problems: A Comparison of European Countries and the United States," *Pacific Institute for Research and Evaluation (PIRE)*, 2005. Reproduced by permission.

Reexamining Stereotypes

Do European youth drink less and experience fewer problems than their American counterparts?

Until recently data did not exist to easily answer this question. In comparison with youth in the United States:

A greater percentage of youth from nearly all European countries report drinking in the past 30 days;

For a majority of these European countries, a greater percentage of youth reported having five or more drinks in a row; and

A great majority of the European countries have higher intoxication rates among youth than the United States and less than a quarter had lower rates or equivalent rates to the United States.

Based on this analysis, the comparison of drinking rates and alcohol-related problems among youth in the United States and in European countries does not provide support for elimination of U.S. minimum drinking age laws or for the implementation of programs to teach responsible drinking to youth.

Do youth from Europe drink more responsibly than do youth from the United States?

This question is often raised in the context of the stricter minimum drinking age laws in the United States. Although the implementation of the uniform minimum drinking age of 21 and the enactment of zero tolerance laws have reduced drinking by youth and saved thousands of lives, these policies have come under attack as contributing to irresponsible styles of drinking. Commonly, European countries are held up as examples of where more liberal drinking age laws and attitudes may foster more responsible styles of drinking by youth. It often is asserted that alcohol is more integrated into European culture and that youth there learn to drink at younger ages within the context of the family. It is further asserted that young Europeans learn to drink more responsibly than do youth from the United States.

This report addresses the question of whether youth in Europe actually drink more responsibly than those in the United States. Data for this paper come from the 2003 European School Survey Project on Alcohol and Other Drugs (ESPAD) and the 2003 United States Monitoring the Future Survey (MTF).

Prevalence of Drinking in the Past 30 Days

The percentage of youth in 35 European countries and the United States reported that they had at least one drink of an alcoholic beverage during the past 30 days. These 30-day prevalence rates are often used as an indicator of the number of current or regular drinkers in a population. In the 2003 MTF survey, 35 percent of 10th graders reported that they had a drink in the past 30 days. The United States is a low consumption country by European standards. With the exception of Turkey (20%), every European country in the ESPAD survey had higher prevalence rates. In most cases, the rates of current drinking far exceeded those observed in the United States. Iceland (37%) and the United States had essentially equivalent prevalence rates on this measure.

Prevalence of Heavy Drinking

Although the data shows that fewer American adolescents are current drinkers than is the case for a vast majority of European countries, it is not clear if the patterns of drinking are such that European adolescents are more at risk for problems. It may be, for example, that more of them drink, but do so moderately in a family context. Consuming five or more drinks in a row is one measure of heavy episodic or "binge" drinking that is frequently used. This style of drinking is known to be associated with increased risk for a number of problems including DUI [driving under the influence], fighting, truancy, and involvement in criminal activities such as theft, burglary, and assault. If the early socialization to drinking that is assumed to be typical of Europe is such that it fosters responsible drinking, then we would expect to see much lower rates of binge drinking there than in the United States. Contrary to these expectations, U.S. adolescents show lower prevalence rates for drinking five or more drinks in a row than most European countries in the ESPAD survey. In many cases, the percentage of youth reporting drinking five or more drinks in a row is considerably higher than that for the United States. Only Turkey (15%) has a substantially lower rate than is seen for the United States (22%). It should be noted that the rates for the United States are lower than those for Italy (34%) or Greece (39%), countries that could be considered typically southern European.

As with binge drinking, intoxication is associated with a wide variety of personal and social problems.

Intoxication

Another measure of problematic drinking is intoxication. Unlike the measures of binge drinking, the items addressing intoxication were identical between the ESPAD and MTF surveys. Thus, direct comparisons can be made with certainty. As with binge drinking, intoxication is associated with a wide variety of personal and social problems. To the extent that the more liberal policies and attitudes toward drinking in Europe contribute to a more responsible drinking style among adolescents, one would expect to find lower rates of intoxication among young Europeans. As with binge drinking, adolescents from the United States show a moderate rate of intoxication (18%) compared with their European peers. The United States is somewhat higher on this measure than some countries (e.g., Cyprus, France, Greece, Portugal, Romania, Turkey), substantially lower than others (e.g., Austria, Denmark, Finland,

Greenland, Ireland, Isle of Man, United Kingdom), and essentially equivalent to still others (e.g., Italy, Malta). Only for Turkey and Cyprus are the prevalence rates substantially lower than for the United States. There is no evidence that the stricter laws and policies regarding drinking by youth in the United States are associated with higher rates of intoxication. Equally, there is no evidence that the more liberal policies and drinking socialization practices in Europe are associated with lower levels of intoxication.

Data Debunk the Myth

Recent data from representative surveys provide no evidence that young Europeans drink more responsibly than their counterparts in the United States.

A greater percentage of youth from nearly all European countries in the survey report drinking in the past 30 days.

For a majority of these European countries, a greater percentage of youth report having five or more drinks in a row compared to U.S. 10th graders. Only for Turkey did a lower percentage of youth report this behavior.

A great majority of the European countries in the survey had higher prevalence rates for self-reported intoxication than the United States, less than a quarter had lower rates, and less than a quarter had rates that were more or less the same as the United States.

9

Education and Police and Community Support Are Necessary

Ralph DiMatteo

Ralph DiMatteo is a certified alcohol awareness trainer.

If young adults are treated as mature people they will behave as such. Instead of solving the problem of binge drinking and drunk driving, the legal drinking age of twenty-one denies people who are old enough to get married, drive, and vote, the opportunity to learn how to drink responsibly. With a better educational approach, police outreach programs, and parent and community guidance, young adults can learn how to drink without the dangers of illegal abuse.

Let me start by saying that since I am a 14-year independent Alcohol Awareness Consultant, I feel that this is definitely a topic I am more than qualified to weigh in on, and if that isn't enough I also have a 25+ year background in the wholesale beer business to boot, and during that time I was the community Responsibility Initiative Designee for Miller Brewing Company for the Cleveland market.

So as you might imagine, I have been following the debate . . . about lowering the legal drinking age from 21 to 18 because of the movement being championed by John McCardell,

Ralph DiMatteo, "Should the Legal Drinking Age Be Reduced to 18?" *Associated Content*, July 20, 2007. Copyright © Associated Content, Inc. Reproduced by permission. Accessed online August 20, 2007, at www.associatedcontent.com/article/313149/ should_the_legal_drinking_age_be_reduced.html.

the president emeritus of Middlebury College in Vermont. McCardell's efforts are based upon the fact the epidemic that is underage and or binge drinking is proof that the current approach is not effective or working. For these reasons, McCardell feels it is time for the United States to bring back the 18-year old drinking age.

Drinking Licenses Might Be Successful

What caught my particular attention about McCardell's reasoning is that he proposes a system that issues drinking "licenses" that would only be issued after someone under the age of 21 would have completed mandatory education about alcohol consumption and its risks, which is pretty much what I do, so I believe he is definitely on the right track, but I would take it one step further, and that is to keep the mandatory education from being too "preachy" or filled with "scare tactics" or statistics. Simply put, if presented properly, and these young adults are indeed treated like adults they will respond as adults accordingly. I know because that is how I train [students in] the University specific program of the TIPS [Training for Intervention Procedures] Alcohol Awareness program. . . .

Armed with factual information . . . [young people] will respond accordingly.

The University specific program is almost always taught to leaders on their campuses from the various Greek organizations [sororities and fraternities] and Student Orientation Committees, and I must admit as I began training this version, I really expected to have the material be met with skepticism and negativity. Frankly I am pleasantly surprised every single time as these young men and women are simply trying to learn more about alcohol so that they do make responsible decisions. What I have come to realize is that if they [are] armed with factual information as opposed to scare tactics, they will respond accordingly.

At Akron University, Bowling Green University, Wittenberg and the University of Pittsburgh at Johnstown . . . I not only have been invited to train the program material, but also to help develop responsible party planning guidelines as these student leaders want their fellow students to make good decisions.

Although statistics show, according to Federal highway crash data from the country, that the raising of the legal drinking age to 21 has saved nearly 25,000 lives over the last 30 years, I still feel that by having a "gap" in the ages of when the law classifies someone as an adult and when the law says that that adult can consume alcohol drives illegal drinking activities "behind closed doors" where they most certainly have no chance of being responsible. . . .

So while I am encouraging you to look further into John McCardell's efforts on your own, I am going to offer up suggestions to ensure that if the legal drinking age is ever reduced to 18 from 21, the likelihood that it would be successful would be greater if some simple steps are followed.

Information Must Replace Taboo

First, the mandatory education that McCardell suggest[s] for under 21 drinking license must come from a credible source such as the TIPS program that is based upon proper serving and selling practices, information about how alcohol affects individuals, and most importantly how to effectively intervene when someone has overconsumed to prevent them from harming themselves or others. Simply putting forth information without support on how to apply it will fail miserably as programs of this kind are only as effective as their implementation.

Second, it is important to invite into the training sessions those within the surrounding college community that offer alcohol ... so that they feel less like part of the problem, and more part of the solution. This will also ensure a "sameness" in presentation and understanding of the material.

If law enforcement is involved from the start they are much more likely to respond to situations to help.

Third, invite local law enforcement and media representatives into the class to not only participate in the class itself but to help spread the word about the responsibility initiatives that will be in place going forward. If law enforcement is involved from the start they are much more likely to respond to situations to help, as opposed to enforce, and media sources exposed to prevention practices are very likely to champion those causes, which is goodwill within the community.

Teach, don't Preach.

Lastly, I said it earlier, but it is worth wrapping up with, "Teach, don't Preach." Young adults treated like adults will surprise you with how much they really do want to do the right thing, they just have to be told what and why about the right thing, and "each will respond according to their own gifts", which, if you're a *Star Trek* fan, you will recognize as a quote from *Star Trek II* spoken by Spock to Kirk about the trainees on the Enterprise. ... I don't know, I think it makes sense, don't you?

10

Lowering the Legal Drinking Age Will Reduce Alcohol's Allure

Ruth Ann Dailey

Ruth Ann Dailey is a staff writer for the Pittsburgh Post-Gazette.

Laws have driven young drinkers underground, banning an otherwise socially acceptable behavior. In a world in which many adults depend on prescription drugs to alleviate stress, depression, and other ailments, teenagers are turning to alcohol, never having learned how to drink responsibly. Lowering the drinking age can bring many adolescents back into social situations where they can experiment with alcohol under the supervision of peers and adults. This will cut down on abuse and destructive binge drinking.

If we want to stop the alarming rise in the number of high school and college kids abusing alcohol and drugs, we have to figure out first why they're doing it.

Chances are pretty good the fault lies with us grown-ups, but not necessarily, or only, for the reasons we might first assume.

Mt. Lebanon [Pennsylvania] District Judge Blaise Larotonda spoke out last week about the serious upswing in underage drinking arrests in his district. The numbers nearly

Ruth Ann Dailey, "Lower Legal Drinking Age to 18," *Pittsburgh Post-Gazette*, March 22, 2007. Copyright, Pittsburgh Post-Gazette, 2007. All rights reserved. Reprinted with permission.

doubled from 2005 to 2006, rising from 106 to 199. The first two months of 2007 have already seen 51 arrests.

Commenting on some parents' worries that no-partying rules will make them hypocrites or harm their kids' social lives, Judge Larotonda said, "Sorry. You're a parent. That's what your job is." Amen to that.

Forty-nine percent of full-time college students abuse drugs or alcohol or both.

But the numbers don't improve once the kids are out of their parents' houses. In Feb. 2007 Columbia University released a study showing that 49 percent of full-time college students abuse drugs or alcohol or both.

While the share of the college population engaging in this behavior is no greater than in 1993, the frequency of their bingeing has increased, including a 26 percent rise in the number of students who get drunk at least three times a month.

Alcohol Is Used as a Cure-all

Let's set aside abuse of illegal or prescription drugs, and limit ourselves to asking, "Why are so many kids heavy drinkers?" Maybe, in part, for the same reasons their parents are. It's self-medication, a liquid fix for anxiety, depression, alienation or despair: You name it, alcohol will help you forget it.

But the study also shows that 23 percent of full-time students meet the medical threshold for substance abuse or dependence—2 1/2 times the rate in the general population. Our kids aren't just drinking like we do, they're drinking much more than we do, and most of them are under age.

The next logical question is: Are we adults fostering unhealthy attitudes toward alcohol among our young people? Other studies support my hunch that we are, especially when considered alongside recent history.

Here's the thumbnail sketch: Until Prohibition was enacted in 1919, drinking was not regulated. When Prohibition was repealed in 1933, most states established a minimum drinking age of 21.

In 1970, the 26th Amendment lowered the voting age to 18, a change that coincided with the Vietnam War and the draft for all men 18 and older. This redefinition of American adulthood led to the familiar complaint: "I'm old enough to vote and go to war but not to discuss it over a beer?"

By 1974, 29 states had lowered their drinking age to 18, but differences from state to state led to border-crossing and a rise in teenage drunk-driving. By the mid '80s the federal government stepped in to mandate 21 as the national standard.

Indiana University professor Ruth Engs released a 1989 study showing that young adults' alcohol abuse actually increased markedly after the nationwide raising of the drinking age. In 20 years of studies, she's repeatedly found that significantly more underage drinkers than college students of legal age are heavy drinkers. These findings underscore the truth of human nature that making something forbidden increases its allure.

When Columbia University released its recent study, Joseph Califano, former U.S. secretary of health, education and welfare, accused college officials of being "Pontius Pilates" who have "facilitated a college culture of alcohol and drug abuse."

Drinking Is Driven Underground

On the contrary, the bravest and wisest educators are pointing out that "latter-day prohibitionists" have driven drinking underground, making it more attractive and more dangerous.

University of Colorado–Boulder Chancellor Roderic Park proposed a return to the lower drinking age as early as 1996, advocating a system of education and permits that mirrors our approach to driving. Middlebury (Vermont) College President John McCardell wrote an essay for *The New York Times* in 2004 arguing that "colleges should be given the chance to educate students, who in all other respects are adults, in the appropriate use of alcohol."

That's how it was when I attended college in the early 1980s. University officials chaperoned "social mixers" where beer was available. I was still a teetotaller then, and the most responsible drinker I knew was the friend who'd had wine at her parents' dinner table since her early teens.

We'll never get rid of all substance abuse.

Statistics from other cultures bear out the benefits of moderation. A recent European Union study reveals that the countries where moderate daily drinking is the norm (Italy, Spain and France) have the fewest binge drinkers (2 percent, 2 percent and 8 percent, compared to 34 percent in Ireland and 27 percent in Finland).

We'll never get rid of all substance abuse. But if we adopt a more reasonable approach to alcohol and adulthood, we can eliminate much of the drinking born of simple defiance and focus our attention on the kids who really need help: the ones drinking to escape mental, emotional or spiritual problems. They deserve better than what we've given.

11

Adults Who Undermine the Legal Drinking Age Should Be Punished

Rebecca Kanable

Rebecca Kanable is a writer specializing in law enforcement topics.

Laws against underage drinking cannot be successful if the public ignores obvious breaches and parents provide alcohol for their teenagers. Youth drinking is not only a health problem, it also can lead to serious crimes. The attitude toward underage drinking has to change if we want to save lives, and the enforcement of the minimum legal drinking age (MLDA) has to be a top priority.

High school students sit around a bonfire drinking beer. Young college students gather at a house known for loud drinking parties. A very young-looking person walks out of a liquor store with a tall bottle disguised in a brown paper bag.

If you come across any of these things happening in your community, what do you do? And, after finding out what your reaction was, how will your community react? If you enforce the law, will the community champion or ridicule your actions? If you look the other way and avoid a lot of paperwork and hassle, will the community be disappointed or thankful?

Underage drinking often seems to be a rite of passage. Eighty-three percent of adults who drink had their first drink

Rebecca Kanable, "Turning Off the Tap: Targeting Adults Who Violate MLDA Laws Stops the Flow of Alcohol to Youth and Prevents Other Problems," *Law Enforcement Technology*, vol. 32, September 2005, p. 80–87. Copyright 2005 Cygnus Business Media. All rights reserved. Reproduced by permission.

of alcohol before age 21, according to the National Center on Addiction and Substance Abuse report on underage drinking released in February 2002.

James Fell, director of Traffic Safety and Enforcement Programs at the Pacific Institute for Research and Evaluation (PIRE) in Calverton, Maryland, compares today's overall attitude toward underage drinking in the United States to the attitude people had toward drunk driving in the 1960s and 1970s—it's tolerated. Not by everyone, he says, but a lot of people don't think underage drinking is a big deal.

Maybe if it's just one beer and no one gets in a car to drive home, underage drinking really isn't that much of a problem. Besides, aren't there more important things law enforcement officers should be doing than tracking down kids soaking up a few suds?

Underage Drinking Leads to Other Crimes

Responding to that devil's advocate thinking, Fell says "no," not in the sense that underage drinking is a huge public health problem that leads to youth endangering others and themselves. Underage drinking can lead to traffic deaths, suicides, homicides, unintentional injuries, assaults, rapes, alcohol dependence, vandalism and property damage—in addition to alcohol poisoning.

With underage drinking, one crime often leads to another.

The effects of youth drinking alcohol can include long-term damage. Current research by the National Institutes of Health Institute of Mental Health and UCLA's [University of California–Los Angeles's] Laboratory of Neuro Imaging shows the brain is not fully developed until about age 25. Early and excessive drinking at an early age can cause irreversible brain damage. Drinking before age 15 has been shown to cause problems in the future (from addiction, to drunk driving and assaults).

With underage drinking, one crime often leads to another.

"If you look at most communities, underage drinking is probably causing more problems than murders, robberies, burglaries, you name it," Fell says, noting exceptions might be found in communities that have a bigger problem with illegal drugs.

In the prevention of underage drinking and related problems, law enforcement plays a key role. A movement exists to re-target law enforcement efforts toward adults that illegally sell or provide alcohol to kids, says Traci Toomey, director of the Alcohol Epidemiology Program within the School of Public Health at the University of Minnesota in Minneapolis. "It is unlikely we have enough resources to create a deterrent effect by targeting underage drinkers," she says. "It is more likely we have enough resources to deter adults violating the minimum legal drinking age (MLDA) laws."

Attitudes Toward Underage Drinking

Alcohol is a drug, the No. 1 drug of choice among children and adolescents, reminds Fell, who serves on the National Board of Directors for Mothers Against Drunk Driving (MADD). If a community, and subsequently, the community's law enforcement officers don't see underage drinking as a big deal, he says, the first step to underage drinking prevention needs to be an attitude change.

The National Academy of Sciences Institute of Medicine's 2003 "Underage Drinking: A Collective Responsibility" says: "There are signs that public attention to underage drinking is increasing and the public recognizes the need to address the problem more aggressively than has thus far occurred."

Specifically the report gives examples as stated below:

(1) A recent study on public attitudes toward underage drinking by A.C. Wagenaar et al., with the University of Minnesota–Minneapolis, shows almost universal recognition of this problem. In fact, 98 percent of adults polled said they were concerned about teen drinking and 66 percent said they were "very concerned."

(2) In 1999, MADD added the goal of reducing underage drinking to its mission statement, and its activities and public statements increasingly reflect this focus.

(3) Underage drinking has also won the attention of the spouses of the nation's governors, many of whom have come together to form the Leadership to Keep Children Alcohol Free, in collaboration with the Robert Wood Johnson Foundation (RWJF) and the National Institute on Alcohol Abuse and Alcoholism (NIAAA, part of the National Institutes of Health). In collaboration with the American Medical Association (AMA), the RWJF has also provided long-term support to 12 community- and 10 university-based coalitions with the specific mission of reducing and preventing underage drinking. The AMA has become increasingly active on the issue of underage drinking, calling for tighter regulation of alcohol availability, higher excise taxes, and restrictions on alcohol advertising.

(4) Members of the alcohol industry also have continued their efforts to discourage underage drinking through responsible drinking campaigns and approaches such as server, parent, and youth-oriented education and involvement in prevention efforts on college campuses.

Youth Drinking Is Still a Problem

Yet, the prevalence of underage drinking remains stable. Underage drinking peaked in the late 1970s and stabilized during the last decade at what researchers at the National Institutes of Health say are disturbingly high levels. Since 1975, information about drinking by people 18 years old and younger has been collected by different ongoing national surveys, including the Monitoring the Future study, the Youth Risk Behavior Survey and the National Household Survey on Drug Abuse.

Research also demonstrates when young people drink, they drink to get drunk.

These surveys show that almost 80 percent of adolescents have consumed alcohol by the time they were 12th-graders. Analyses showed a long period of decreases until the early 1990s, and likely the decline reflects the increase in the minimum legal drinking age from 18 to 21.

Research also demonstrates when young people drink, they drink to get drunk.

The data also show that more than 12 percent of 8th-graders and nearly 30 percent of 12th-graders report drinking five or more drinks in a row in the past two weeks.

Among 18 to 22 year olds, 41.4 percent of full-time college students and 35.9 percent of other young adults report heavy drinking (Substance Abuse and Mental Health Services Administration, 2002).

Enforcement of the MLDA

The $61.9 billion-per-year (estimated cost of underage drinking) question is what can be done to stop youth from drinking alcohol.

Can you imagine how many lives would be saved if we enforced the law?

The most effective tactic has been raising the minimum legal drinking age to 21. Because of this law, an estimated 900 to 1,000 lives per year in youth traffic deaths alone are saved, according to the National Highway Traffic Safety Administration [NHTSA](Traffic Safety Facts: Young Drivers, 2003).

"Can you imagine how many lives would be saved if we enforced the law?" asks Fell, who worked at the NHTSA, as chief of research and evaluation for Traffic Safety Programs and manager of the Fatality Analysis Reporting System (FARS).

People think that the 21 drinking age law is the same in every state. The components of the drinking age law actually vary from state to state. There are 17 different components. The highest number of components a state has without loopholes and exceptions is 14, the least is three. Examples of components include: it's illegal for anyone under 21 to consume alcohol, it's illegal to use a fake ID, it's illegal for an adult to furnish alcohol to youth, it's illegal for an alcohol vendor to sell alcohol to youth, and it's illegal for any driver under age 21 to drive with any alcohol in their blood system (zero tolerance). Fell is working on a study looking at what components states have, how well they're enforced and whether enforcement reduces alcohol-related fatalities.

Joel Grube, director of the Prevention Research Center in Berkeley, California, says, "In a lot of ways enforcement is where the rubber hits the road. Law enforcement officers have a very important role to play in making sure the law is enforced because it is an effective prevention strategy."

A study by Grube, who holds a doctorate in social psychology, and Clyde Dent and Anthony Biglan of the Oregon Research Institute in Eugene, provides scientific evidence that underage drinking may be reduced by increasing enforcement of the minimum-age purchase laws and reducing the number of outlets that sell alcohol to kids. They found that underage drinking prevalence was lower in communities where young people perceived greater enforcement of underage drinking laws and where alcohol was more difficult to obtain. Their findings were published in "Community level alcohol availability and enforcement of possession laws as predictors of youth drinking," in the December 2004 "Preventative Medicine."

Compliance Checks

One way to strongly deter sales to minors is police checks of establishments that sell alcohol. Research by Alexander Wagenaar at the University of Florida, and Toomey and Darin Erickson at the University of Minnesota found police checks are even more effective when they are repeated as often as every three months. During the compliance checks, an underage buyer attempts to buy alcohol without showing identification and violators are cited. Researchers found these checks work far better than programs that train bar and restaurant staff to identify and refuse service to minors.

"We found that enforcement has significant effects, but just like enforcement against any offense, you can't just do it once and think it solves everything," says Wagenaar, a professor of epidemiology and health policy research at the University of Florida's College of Medicine. "We have to create an ongoing perception on the part of the managers and owners of these establishments that they have a decent chance of getting caught if they sell to teenagers."

Law enforcement checks of liquor stores and other establishments selling alcohol for off-premise consumption produced an immediate 17-percent decrease in the subsequent likelihood of their selling to minors, researchers say. That reduction dissipated over time, from 11 percent two weeks after a check to 3 percent after two months. Most of the residual effect disappeared after three months.

Checks of bars and other on-premise establishments yielded even better results, with a 17-percent decrease immediately afterward diminishing to 14 percent at two weeks and 11 percent at two months.

Another finding of the research is compliance checks need to be checking all establishments regularly for preventative purposes.

Where kids get alcohol varies by age group, says Toomey. As kids get older, they might be more likely to try to sneak into bars, she says. While kids might have fake IDs, she says the purpose of compliance checks is to make sure establishments are doing the minimum of asking for IDs and checking them.

The study was carried out during a national downward trend in the tendency of alcohol establishments to sell to underage youth. In the early 1990s, the rate was 50 to 80 percent, Wagenaar says. In the research conducted by Wagenaar, Toomey and Erickson, the rate was roughly 20 percent.

"Communities have stepped up enforcement," he says. "There is much more carding going on now than in the '80s and '90s. There has been substantial progress, but most communities still pay way too little attention to enforcing the law against sales of alcohol to minors."

Shoulder Tap Campaigns

In addition to cutting off illegal sales, illegal provision must be cut off, especially since it is a more common means of youth obtaining alcohol, says Toomey, who holds a Ph.D. in epidemiology and is an associate professor.

In the Oregon study, 70 percent of youth got their alcohol from friends, parents or other social sources, while 30 percent got their alcohol from convenience stores, supermarkets or other commercial sources.

Although there is research supporting the effectiveness of compliance checks to cut off illegal sales, Toomey says there are only recommendations for what works to cut off illegal provision.

Shoulder tap campaigns have been effective in some communities. They are similar to compliance checks, but law enforcement has an underage person under their supervision approach an adult. If the adult agrees to purchase alcohol, it's an illegal act and the adult could be fined or arrested provided there are no concerns of entrapment. Or, a warning could be given saying if this had not been an educational campaign, a specific fine or jail term could have been issued.

Keg Registration Laws

Twenty-four states have keg registration laws. (Utah prohibits keg sales.) Retailers put a unique identifier on each keg. When someone purchases the keg, that person's name, driver's license number and other identifying information is recorded with ID number of the keg.

If officers go to a house or an open field where they find a party and underage people drinking, and people flee the scene or no one will admit to purchasing the keg, officers can use the keg ID number to find the buyer and charge this person with illegal provision.

Social providers are often difficult to find, Toomey says. Keg registration is one tool to help locate them.

How do you make people think they're likely to get caught if they provide alcohol to someone under 21?

Education of the Public

How do you make people think they're likely to get caught if they provide alcohol to someone under 21? One way, if someone is arrested, is to make sure there is publicity about the arrest so it can be used as an opportunity to educate other adults, she says.

"I don't think a lot of adults really know what the laws are," says Toomey. "I'm still surprised when people ask if the legal drinking age is 21 in all states."

Whenever possible, she says law enforcement should both enforce and educate. She adds that education needs to go beyond the school setting because education in the schools alone has not sustained reductions in underage alcohol use.

She says in one small community police officers went so far as to visit the home of every high school senior before prom and graduation, and informed students and their parents of the consequences of violating the minimum legal drinking age law.

Other Solutions to Underage Drinking

Other law enforcement tactics found to be effective against underage drinking include false ID detection machines; zero tolerance enforcement (no alcohol for drivers under the age of 21); and sobriety checkpoints, especially checkpoints using passive alcohol sensors. . . .

To bring all the stakeholders together, community coalitions can be formed. For example, Communities Mobilizing for Change on Alcohol (CMCA) is a community organizing effort developed and evaluated by the Alcohol Epidemiology Program at the University of Minnesota. CMCA is designed to change policies and practices of major community institutions in ways that reduce access to alcohol by teenagers. . . .

Minnesota, like other states, has seen change thanks to its coalition, says Toomey, who serves on the National Board of Directors for MADD. In recent years community concerns have led to changes in the form of keg registration, a social host or civil cause of action and funding for compliance checks, she says.

Each community must look at what best fits its needs. Effective enforcement and prevention strategies include enforcing minimum age purchase laws and this can be done in conjunction with

- Compliance checks

- Shoulder tap campaigns

- Keg registration laws

- Education that goes beyond schools

Fell concludes, "There are lots of things that we can do. We just have to get serious about addressing the problem of underage drinking."

12

Early Alcohol Consumption Puts Youth at Risk

National Institute on Alcohol Abuse and Alcoholism

The National Institute on Alcohol Abuse and Alcoholism of the National Institutes of Health provides leadership in the national effort to reduce alcohol-related problems.

Despite a minimum legal drinking age of 21, many young people in the United States consume alcohol. Some abuse alcohol by drinking frequently or by binge drinking—often defined as having five or more drinks in a row. The progression of drinking from use to abuse to dependence is associated with biological and psychosocial factors. This Alcohol Alert bulletin examines some of these factors that put youth at risk for drinking and for alcohol-related problems and considers some of the consequences of their drinking.

Prevalence of Youth Drinking

Thirteen- to fifteen-year-olds are at high risk to begin drinking. According to results of an annual survey of students in 8th, 10th, and 12th grades, 26 percent of 8th graders, 40 percent of 10th graders, and 51 percent of 12th graders reported drinking alcohol within the past month. Binge drinking at least once during the 2 weeks before the survey was reported by 16 percent of 8th graders, 25 percent of 10th graders, and 30 percent of 12th graders.

Males report higher rates of daily drinking and binge drinking than females, but these differences are diminishing.

National Institute on Alcohol Abuse and Alcoholism (NIAAA), "Youth Drinking: Risk Factors and Consequences," *Alcohol Alert*, http://pubs.niaaa.nih.gov/publications/aa37.htm.

White students report the highest levels of drinking, blacks report the lowest, and Hispanics fall between the two.

A survey focusing on the alcohol-related problems experienced by 4,390 high school seniors and dropouts found that within the preceding year, approximately 80 percent reported either getting "drunk," binge drinking, or drinking and driving. More than half said that drinking had caused them to feel sick, miss school or work, get arrested, or have a car crash.

Some adolescents who drink later abuse alcohol and may develop alcoholism. Although these conditions are defined for adults in the DSM [Diagnostic and Statistical Manual of Mental Disorders], research suggests that separate diagnostic criteria may be needed for youth.

While drinking may be a singular problem behavior for some, research suggests that for others it may be an expression of general adolescent turmoil that includes other problem behaviors.

Drinking and Adolescent Development

While drinking may be a singular problem behavior for some, research suggests that for others it may be an expression of general adolescent turmoil that includes other problem behaviors and that these behaviors are linked to unconventionality, impulsiveness, and sensation seeking.

Binge drinking, often beginning around age 13, tends to increase during adolescence, peak in young adulthood (ages 18–22), then gradually decrease. In a 1994 national survey, binge drinking was reported by 28 percent of high school seniors, 41 percent of 21- to 22-year-olds, but only 25 percent of 31- to 32-year-olds. Individuals who increase their binge drinking from age 18 to 24 and those who consistently binge drink at least once a week during this period may have problems attaining the goals typical of the transition from adolescence to young adulthood (e.g., marriage, educational attainment, employment, and financial independence).

Risk Factors for Adolescent Alcohol Use, Abuse, and Dependence

Genetic Risk Factors. Animal studies and studies of twins and adoptees demonstrate that genetic factors influence an individual's vulnerability to alcoholism. Children of alcoholics are significantly more likely than children of nonalcoholics to initiate drinking during adolescence and to develop alcoholism, but the relative influences of environment and genetics have not been determined and vary among people.

Biological Markers. Brain waves elicited in response to specific stimuli (e.g., a light or sound) provide measures of brain activity that predict risk for alcoholism. P300, a wave that occurs about 300 milliseconds after a stimulus, is most frequently used in this research. A low P300 amplitude has been demonstrated in individuals with increased risk for alcoholism, especially sons of alcoholic fathers. P300 measures among 36 preadolescent boys were able to predict alcohol and other drug (AOD) use 4 years later, at an average age of 16.

Childhood Behavior. Children classified as "undercontrolled" (i.e., impulsive, restless, and distractible) at age 3 were twice as likely as those who were "inhibited" or "well-adjusted" to be diagnosed with alcohol dependence at age 21. Aggressiveness in children as young as ages 5–10 has been found to predict AOD use in adolescence. Childhood antisocial behavior is associated with alcohol-related problems in adolescence (24–27) and alcohol abuse or dependence in adulthood.

Psychiatric Disorders. Among 12- to 16-year-olds, regular alcohol use has been significantly associated with conduct disorder; in one study, adolescents who reported higher levels of drinking were more likely to have conduct disorder.

Six-year-old to seventeen-year-old boys with attention deficit hyperactivity disorder (ADHD) who were also found to have weak social relationships had significantly higher rates of alcohol abuse and dependence 4 years later, compared with ADHD boys without social deficiencies and boys without ADHD.

Whether anxiety and depression lead to or are consequences of alcohol abuse is unresolved. In a study of college freshmen, a DSM-III diagnosis of alcohol abuse or dependence was twice as likely among those with anxiety disorder as those without this disorder. In another study, college students diagnosed with alcohol abuse were almost four times as likely as students without alcohol abuse to have a major depressive disorder. In most of these cases, depression preceded alcohol abuse. In a study of adolescents in residential treatment for AOD dependence, 25 percent met the DSM-III-R criteria for depression, three times the rate reported for controls. In 43 percent of these cases, the onset of AOD dependence preceded the depression; in 35 percent, the depression occurred first; and in 22 percent, the disorders occurred simultaneously.

Suicidal Behavior. Alcohol use among adolescents has been associated with considering, planning, attempting, and completing suicide. In one study, 37 percent of eighth-grade females who drank heavily reported attempting suicide, compared with 11 percent who did not drink. Research does not indicate whether drinking causes suicidal behavior, only that the two behaviors are correlated.

Parents' drinking behavior and favorable attitudes about drinking have been positively associated with adolescents' initiating and continuing drinking.

Psychosocial Risk Factors

Parenting, Family Environment, and Peers. Parents' drinking behavior and favorable attitudes about drinking have been positively associated with adolescents' initiating and continuing drinking. Early initiation of drinking has been identified as an important risk factor for later alcohol-related problems. Children who were warned about alcohol by their parents and children who reported being closer to their parents were less likely to start drinking.

Lack of parental support, monitoring, and communication have been significantly related to frequency of drinking, heavy drinking, and drunkenness among adolescents. Harsh, inconsistent discipline and hostility or rejection toward children have also been found to significantly predict adolescent drinking and alcohol-related problems.

Peer drinking and peer acceptance of drinking have been associated with adolescent drinking. While both peer influences and parental influences are important, their relative impact on adolescent drinking is unclear.

Expectancies. Positive alcohol-related expectancies have been identified as risk factors for adolescent drinking. Positive expectancies about alcohol have been found to increase with age (50) and to predict the onset of drinking and problem drinking among adolescents.

Trauma. Child abuse and other traumas have been proposed as risk factors for subsequent alcohol problems. Adolescents in treatment for alcohol abuse or dependence reported higher rates of physical abuse, sexual abuse, violent victimization, witnessing violence, and other traumas compared with controls. The adolescents in treatment were at least 6 times more likely than controls to have ever been abused physically and at least 18 times more likely to have ever been abused sexually. In most cases, the physical or sexual abuse preceded the alcohol use. Thirteen percent of the alcohol dependent adolescents had experienced posttraumatic stress disorder, compared with 10 percent of those who abused alcohol and 1 percent of controls.

Advertising. Research on the effects of alcohol advertising on adolescent alcohol-related beliefs and behaviors has been limited. While earlier studies measured the effects of exposure to advertising, more recent research has assessed the effects of alcohol advertising awareness on intentions to drink. In a study of fifth- and sixth-grade students' awareness, measured by the ability to identify products in commercials with the product name blocked out, awareness had a small but statistically significant relationship to positive expectancies about alcohol and to intention to drink as adults. This suggests that alcohol advertising may influence adolescents to be more favorably predisposed to drinking.

Consequences of Adolescent Alcohol Use

Drinking and Driving. Of the nearly 8,000 drivers ages 15–20 involved in fatal crashes in 1995, 20 percent had blood alcohol concentrations above zero.

Sexual Behavior. Surveys of adolescents suggest that alcohol use is associated with risky sexual behavior and increased vulnerability to coercive sexual activity. Among adolescents surveyed in New Zealand, alcohol misuse was significantly associated with unprotected intercourse and sexual activity before age 16. Forty-four percent of sexually active Massachusetts teenagers said they were more likely to have sexual intercourse if they had been drinking, and 17 percent said they were less likely to use condoms after drinking.

Risky Behavior and Victimization. Survey results from a nationally representative sample of 8th and 10th graders indicated that alcohol use was significantly associated with both risky behavior and victimization and that this relationship was strongest among the 8th-grade males, compared with other students.

Puberty and Bone Growth. High doses of alcohol have been found to delay puberty in female and male rats, and large quantities of alcohol consumed by young rats can slow bone growth and result in weaker bones. However, the implications of these findings for young people are not clear.

13

Teenage Party Trips Encourage Underage Drinking

Tamara Jones

Tamara Jones is a feature writer at The Washington Post.

Many travel agencies cater to adolescents and young adults under the age of twenty-one, taking them on tours to resort towns where the legal drinking age is eighteen, and the laws are not enforced. Even trustworthy teens can be tempted by inexpensive alcohol, sometimes with catastrophic results. Instead of hoping for the best, parents should take a more active role and accompany their teens on group trips.

It was supposed to be high school's last hurrah, a big blowout with friends at the end of senior year, before everyone scattered to different colleges. Destination: Cancun, Mexico, where the beaches are beautiful, the nightclubs are rowdy, and the legal drinking age is 18.

The trip wasn't until June, but Laurie had started badgering her parents for permission in the fall. She'd work and earn the money herself! The place was fine—it was a tourist resort! Her friends were going! She'd be 18 by then, anyway. Didn't they trust her? Reluctantly, her parents gave in.

A Town Free of Parents

As soon as she hit Cancun, Laurie discovered a scene familiar to anyone who's ever turned on MTV: The town's strip was teeming with teens looking for a good time. Free of parents,

Tamara Jones, "Will Your Teen Be Safe on a Party Trip? Unlike Natalee Holloway, Most Kids Don't Disappear on Spring-Break or Graduation Trips—But They do Face Some Dangers. So Before you Give in to Their Pleas, Read This." *Good Housekeeping*, vol. 242, February 2006, p. 102–106. Copyright © 2006 Hearst Communications, Inc. Reproduced by permission of the author.

in a place where tequila was as available as soda, her friends sought nightspots where they could binge-drink easily and cheaply. Popular tourist bars hosted parties for American teens on a variety of package trips; teens who'd bought "VIP" wristbands (from the club, the bar, or sometimes their own tour organizers) were entitled to 12 drinks for ten bucks. But kids didn't have to be on a tour to find plenty of action, as Laurie and her friends soon learned. In bars throbbing with hormonally charged kids, girls were encouraged to dance atop bars and even to simulate oral sex acts. Some who were just bystanders were drenched with pitchers of beer by guys wanting to see through their tops. For the first few nights, Laurie tried to keep up, drinking until she passed out.

One night, she decided she'd had enough. After her friends refused to leave a club, Laurie set off for the hotel alone. Walking seemed safer than taking a taxi by herself, and she tried to ignore the heckling of men on the street. Suddenly she heard footsteps. Terrified that she was being followed, she raced to the hotel. Back in her room, sobbing, she picked up the phone and called her parents: "I need to get out of here!" They immediately bought her a full-price plane ticket home.

Mitru Ciarlante, who told Laurie's story to *Good Housekeeping*, was disturbed by what had happened to the girl but not surprised. As program associate of the teen victim initiative at the National Center for Victims of Crime, she knows too well that teens on "party trips" face many potential dangers, from alcohol poisoning to date rape and STDs [sexually transmitted diseases]. These kinds of spring-break and graduation vacations often involve teens flashing bare breasts, passing out drunk, and living by the motto "What happens in Cancun, stays in Cancun." A similar scene can be found in other foreign beach resorts—Puerto Vallarta [Mexico], Acapulco [Mexico], or the Bahamas, for example—as well as in American destinations like South Padre Island, Texas, and Panama City and Daytona Beach, Florida.

These teen trips have become so popular (and lucrative for organizers) that several tour companies now have divisions specifically for high schoolers. Promoters like Inertia Tours and Invasion (a division of Student Adventure Travel) offer vacations for less than $1,000, payable in installments—well within reach of a kid with a part-time job. An estimated 100,000 kids—most of them 17 to 19 years old—go on some type of package trip each year, whether they sign up with a tour organizer or simply grab a group of pals, as Laurie did, and arrange a little package of their own, getting a good combination deal on flights and a hotel through an airline or a travel agent. Most return home safely, having experienced nothing worse than a bad hangover, but there are exceptions. The most notable: 18-year-old Natalee Holloway of Alabama, who, as we went to press, had not returned from her post-graduation trip to Aruba last May [2005]. Now that spring break 2006 is close at hand, perhaps more parents should ask the question, Do I know everything that's involved in teen party trips—and can my child really handle all this?

Danger in Paradise

For parents, a graduation trip often focused on a tour of museums in our nation's capital. Nowadays, teen trips are about "parties, craziness, letting go," says Amy, a Maryland teen who requested anonymity because, though her parents allowed her to go to Cancun in 2005, "they don't know everything that went on."

On these trips, access to alcohol is a big draw. At 17, Amy was underage even in Mexico, but she says that none of the staff members on her tour tried to keep her from drinking. The nightclubs never carded her, and she was able to buy a wristband entitling her to drinks for a dollar each.

Kirk Riley, president of Student Adventure Travel, says his company's trips for high school students are nonalcoholic, meaning that his staff doesn't sell drinks, and the company's tour materials point out that the drinking age in Mexico is 18. "Still, we can't prevent the kids from getting wristbands," says Riley.

Underage drinking also takes place on teen trips within U.S. borders. "There are tons of fake IDs," reports Nancy, 18, of Ontario, Canada, who spent spring break last year on a trip to Daytona Beach.

For kids on trips, sex is another attraction. "You're there to hook up," says Amy. "That's what sells the place." Last year, on a postgraduation trip to Panama City, Rebecca, an 18-year-old from Tennessee, was horrified to find that "girls I'd been friends with forever were bringing home two and three guys a night—just guys they'd met at the beach." She even caught one friend having sex with a stranger on a balcony. "These girls had always been a little wild, but not like this," she adds.

Alcohol fuels the fire. "Don't paint this as Sodom and Gomorrah. These are good kids," says Mark Engelman, M.D., founder and president of AmeriMed, a chain of American hospitals in Mexico. "But a few kids will always drink themselves into comas or aspirate vomit." And then there are the tragedies—in Dr. Engelman's words, "someone who's drunk or drugged and decides to dive from a hotel balcony into the swimming pool. Every year, some kid goes home paralyzed. Every. Single. Year."

Alcohol also increases the chances of sexual assault.

Alcohol also increases the chances of sexual assault. "The message society sends is that anybody at a 'girls gone wild' knows what to expect," says Ciarlante. "And that puts guys at risk for behaving in a way they usually wouldn't." Parents who decide they'd like solid safety information before deciding about a trip are out of luck—there's no reliable record of trip-related accidents or assaults. Police reports in foreign countries can be spotty, and crimes like date rape often go unreported.

"Staff" Versus "Chaperone"

In light of these dangers, parents may conclude that tour companies are the safest bet, since they have staff members on duty 24-7. However, that may not mean what you think it means. "We have staff members at the hotel and all our events," says Student Adventure Travel's Riley. Their role? "To greet customers, host a safety orientation, and organize activities." Translation: Staffers are there to assist, not to supervise. In its trip materials, Invasion states: "Our staff are there to help you out if you have problems, not to babysit you like chaperones."

Neither Invasion nor Inertia imposes curfews or room checks. Tour activities (which range from snorkeling to bar nights) are all voluntary, so teens spend hours away from staffers. There are rules—no drugs, no fighting, no destroying hotel property—and a teen who breaks them may have privileges revoked or even be sent home early. Chad Hart of Inertia argues that his company's staff support is better than traditional chaperonage. "Parents go to the nightclub," he says, "but they get tired and leave, thinking 'The kids will be OK alone here. It's only a block from the hotel.'" In contrast, he says, Inertia posts staffers "inside and outside the club at every event," and one of their duties is to stop any group member from leaving a bar alone or with strangers.

Hart sees the Holloway disappearance as proof that more personal supervision doesn't guarantee safety either. Seven adults—mostly coaches and their wives, says Holloway's aunt, Marcia Twitty—accompanied more than 120 students on the privately planned trip. Twitty calls the chaperones "wonderful people. . . . We trust them to this day." And yet, Natalee left a club with three local guys the night she disappeared. Twitty's bottom line: "We did not expect [the adults] to be babysitters. They were there to help the kids."

Parents Need to Be Worried

Despite the Holloway case, parents aren't as worried about these trips as they should be, suggests Brett Sokolow, head of the National Center for Higher Education Risk Management. "There's tremendous parent apathy on the topic," he says. When he addresses moms and dads about spring-break safety, the usual attendance is only ten to 20—out of a senior class of 1,000.

Another reason parents sometimes give permission: "It's hard to be the only mom or dad to say no—and then to deal with the wrath of your teenagers on top of it," says Kennesaw, Georgia, family therapist Michael Popkin, Ph.D., author of *Active Parenting of Teens.* When his own 17-year-old daughter wanted to go to Aruba with friends, he and other parents offered a compromise: four days in Nassau, with one responsible adult accompanying each student. The kids accepted the deal.

Kitty Schmitt of San Clemente, California, gave daughter Caitlyn, 18, permission to go on a group trip to Cabo San Lucas [Mexico]—but only if she agreed to certain conditions. "Never go off on your own," Schmitt told her. "Ever. Even if you're just leaving the beach to get a soda, take a friend."

But some parents feel that group trips are no longer worth the risk. Michelle Richardson, a 39-year-old single mom in Gaithersburg, Maryland, is sure her daughter Teddy, 17, will lobby to join friends on spring break. And Richardson has her answer: no. "Teddy will say 'Mom, don't you trust me?' But I'll tell her what I tell other parents: I've only got one shot at this, and I'm going to do it to the best of my ability. If that makes you unhappy or makes me unpopular, I'm cool with that."

14

Teenage Driving Is as Dangerous as Teenage Drinking

Anna Quindlen

Anna Quindlen is the author of five novels, two children's books, and seven nonfiction books. Her New York Times *editorial column, "Public and Private" won the Pulitzer Prize in 1992. Her column now appears semimonthly in* Newsweek.

While the legal drinking age has received much attention and has been at the middle of a recurring debate over its virtues, the legal driving age has been neglected. The risks of adolescent driving by far outweigh those of adolescent drinking. Parents appreciate their children's mobility, but they are closing their eyes to the number one killer of teenagers in the country.

The four years of high school grind inexorably to a close, the milestones passed. The sports contests, the SATs [Scholastic Assessment Tests], the exams, the elections, the dances, the proms. And too often, the funerals. It's become a sad rite of passage in many American communities, the services held for teenagers killed in auto accidents before they've even scored a tassel to hang from the rearview mirror. The hearse moves in procession followed by the late-model compact cars of young people, boys trying to control trembling lower lips and girls sobbing into one another's shoulders. The yearbook

Anna Quindlen, "Driving to the Funeral: If Someone Told You That There Was One Behavior Most Likely to Lead to the Premature Death of Your Kid, Wouldn't You Do Something About That?," *Newsweek*, vol. 80, June 11, 2007, p. 80. Copyright © 2007 Newsweek, Inc. Reproduced by permission.

has a picture or two with a black border. A mom and dad rise from their seats on the athletic field or in the gym to accept a diploma posthumously.

It's simple and inarguable: car crashes are the No. 1 cause of death among 15- to 20-year-olds in this country.

It's simple and inarguable: car crashes are the No. 1 cause of death among 15- to 20-year-olds in this country. What's so peculiar about that fact is that so few adults focus on it until they are planning an untimely funeral. Put it this way: if someone told you that there was one single behavior that would be most likely to lead to the premature death of your kid, wouldn't you try to do something about that? Yet parents seem to treat the right of a 16-year-old to drive as an inalienable one, something to be neither questioned nor abridged.

Young Teen Driving Age Only Benefits Parents

This makes no sense unless the argument is convenience, and often it is. In a nation that developed mass-transit amnesia and traded the exurb for the small town, a licensed son or daughter relieves parents of a relentless roundelay of driving. Soccer field, Mickey Ds, mall, movies. Of course, if that's the rationale, why not let 13-year-olds drive? Any reasonable person would respond that a 13-year-old is too young. But statistics suggest that that's true of 16-year-olds as well. The National Highway Traffic Safety Administration has found that neophyte drivers of 17 have about a third as many accidents as their counterparts only a year younger.

In 1984 a solution was devised for the problem of teenage auto accidents that lulled many parents into a false sense of security. The drinking age was raised from 18 to 21. It's become gospel that this has saved thousands of lives, although no one actually knows if that's the case; fatalities fell, but the use of seat belts and airbags may have as much to do with that as penalties for alcohol use. And there has been a pronounced negative effect on college campuses, where administrators describe a forbidden-fruit climate that encourages binge drinking. The pitchers of sangria and kegs of beer that offered legal refreshment for 18-year-olds at sanctioned campus events 30 years ago have given way to a new tradition called "pre-gaming," in which dry college activities are preceded by manic alcohol consumption at frats, dorms and bars.

Raising the Drinking Age Was Not the Solution

Given the incidence of auto-accident deaths among teenagers despite the higher drinking age, you have to ask whether the powerful lobby Mothers Against Drunk Driving simply targeted the wrong D. In a survey of young drivers, only half said they had seen a peer drive after drinking. Nearly all, however, said they had witnessed speeding, which is the leading factor in fatal crashes by teenagers today. In Europe, governments are relaxed about the drinking age but tough on driving regulations and licensing provisions; in most countries, the driving age is 18.

Perhaps the only ones who wouldn't make a fuss [about raising the legal driving age] are those parents who have accepted diplomas at graduation because their children were no longer alive to do so themselves.

In America some states have taken a tough-love position and bumped up the requirements for young drivers: longer permit periods, restrictions or bans on night driving. Since the greatest danger to a teenage driver is another teenager in the car—the chance of having an accident doubles with two teenage passengers and skyrockets with three or more—some new rules forbid novice drivers from transporting their peers.

In theory this sounds like a good idea; in fact it's toothless. New Jersey has some of the most demanding regulations for new drivers in the nation, including a provision that until they are 18 they cannot have more than one nonfamily member in the car. Yet in early January three students leaving school in Freehold Township died in a horrific accident in which the car's 17-year-old driver was violating that regulation by carrying two friends. No wonder he took the chance: between July 2004 and November 2006, only 12 provisional drivers were ticketed for carrying too many passengers. Good law, bad enforcement.

States Should Raise the Driving Age

States might make it easier on themselves, on police officers and on teenagers, too, if instead of chipping away at the right to drive they merely raised the legal driving age wholesale. There are dozens of statistics to back up such a change: in Massachusetts alone, one third of 16-year-old drivers have been involved in serious accidents. Lots and lots of parents will tell you that raising the driving age is untenable, that the kids need their freedom and their mobility. Perhaps the only ones who wouldn't make a fuss are those parents who have accepted diplomas at graduation because their children were no longer alive to do so themselves, whose children traded freedom and mobility for their lives. They might think it was worth the wait.

Organizations to Contact

The editors have compiled the following list of organizations concerned with the issues debated in this book. The descriptions are derived from materials provided by the organizations. All have publications or information available for interested readers. The list was compiled on the date of publications of the present volume; the information provided here may change. Be aware that many organizations may take several weeks or longer to respond to inquiries, so allow as much time as possible.

Al-Anon Family Group Headquarters

1600 Corporate Landing Pkwy., Virginia Beach, VA   23454
(757) 563-1600 • fax: (757) 563-1655
Web site: www.al/anon.alateen.org

Al-Anon is a fellowship of men, women, and children whose lives have been affected by an alcoholic family member or friend. Members share their experiences, strength, and hope to help each other and perhaps to aid in the recovery of the alcoholic. Al-Anon Family Group Headquarters provides information on its local chapters and on its affiliated organization, Alateen. Its publications include the monthly magazine the *Forum*, the semiannual *Al-Anon Speaks Out*, the bimonthly *Alateen Talk*, and several books, including *How Al-Anon Works, Path to Recovery Steps, Traditions, and Concepts,* and *Courage to Be Me: Living with Alcoholism.*

Alcoholics Anonymous (AA)

General Service Office, PO Box 4
Grand Central Station, New York, NY   10163
(212) 870-3400 • fax: (212) 870-3003
Web site: www.aa.org

AA is an international fellowship of people who are recovering from alcoholism. Because AA's primary goal is to help alcoholics remain sober, it does not sponsor research or engage in education about alcoholism. AA does, however, publish a catalog of literature concerning the organization as well as several pamphlets, including *Is AA for You? Young People and AA*, and *A Brief Guide to Alcoholics Anonymous.*

Canadian Centre on Substance Abuse/Centre canadien de lutte contre l'alcoolisme et les toxicomanies (CCSA/CCLAT)

75 Albert St., Suite 300, Ottawa, ON
   K1P 5E7
   Canada
(800) 244-4788 • fax: (613) 235-8101
Web site: www.ccsa.ca

A Canadian clearinghouse on substance abuse, the CCSA/CCLAT works to disseminate information on the nature, extent, and consequences of substance abuse and to support and assist organizations involved in substance abuse treatment, prevention, and educational programming. The CCSA/CCLAT publishes several books, including *Canadian Profile: Alcohol, Tobacco, and Other Drugs*, as well as reports, policy documents, brochures, research papers, and the newsletter *Action News.*

Centre for Addiction and Mental Health/Centre de toxicomanie at de sante mentale (CAMH)

33 Russell St., Toronto, ON
   M5S 2S1
   Canada
(416) 535-8501
Web site: www.camh.net

CAMH is a public hospital and the largest addiction facility in Canada. It also functions as a research facility, an education and training center, and a community-based organization providing health and addiction prevention services throughout Ontario, Canada. Further, CAMH is a Pan American Health Organization and World Health Organization Collaborating Centre. CAMH publishes the quarterly *CrossCurrents*, the *Journal of Addiction and Mental Health* and offers free alcoholism prevention literature that can either be downloaded or ordered on the Web site.

Choose Responsibility
PO Box 507, Middlebury, VT   05753
(802) 398-2024
e-mail: info@chooseresponsibility.org
Web site: www.chooseresponsibility.org

Choose Responsibility is a nonprofit organization founded to stimulate informed and dispassionate public discussion about the presence of alcohol in American culture and to consider policies that will effectively empower young adults age eighteen to twenty to make mature decisions regarding alcohol use. The Web site offers information about the history of the minimum legal drinking age, as well as links to other organizations dealing with the issue.

Distilled Spirits Council of the United States (DISCUS)
1250 I St. NW, Suite 900, Washington, DC   20005
(202) 628-3544
Web site: www.discus.org

DISCUS is the national trade association representing producers and marketers of distilled spirits in the United States. It seeks to ensure the responsible advertising and marketing of distilled spirits to adult consumers and to prevent such advertising and marketing from targeting individuals below the legal purchase age. DISCUS publishes fact sheets, the newsletter *News Release*, and several pamphlets, including the *Drunk Driving Prevention Act*.

International Center for Alcohol Policies (ICAP)
1519 New Hampshire Ave. NW, Washington, DC   20036
(202) 986-1159 • fax: (202) 986-2080
Web site: www.icap.org

ICAP is a nonprofit organization dedicated to helping reduce the abuse of alcohol worldwide and to promote understanding of the role of alcohol in society through dialogue and partnerships involving the beverage industry, the public health community, and others interested in alcohol policy. ICAP is supported by eleven major international beverage alcohol companies. ICAP publishes reports on pertinent issues such as *Safe Alcohol Consumption, The Limits of Binge Drinking, Health Warning Labels, Drinking Age Limits,* and *Who Are the Abstainers?*

Mothers Against Drunk Driving (MADD)
511 E. John Carpenter Fwy., No. 700, Irving, TX   75062
(800) GET-MADD • fax: (972) 869-2206
e-mail: info@madd.org
Web site: www.madd.org

MADD seeks to act as the voice of victims of drunk driving accidents by speaking on their behalf to communities, businesses, and educational groups, and by providing materials for use in medical facilities and health and driver education programs. MADD publishes the biannual *MADDvocate for Victims Magazine* and the newsletter *MADD in Action* as well as a variety of brochures and other materials on drunk driving.

National Council on Alcoholism and Drug Dependence (NCADD)
12 W. 21st St., New York, NY   10010
(212) 206-6770 • fax: (212) 645-1690
Web site: www.ncadd.org

NCADD is a volunteer health organization that helps individuals overcome addictions, advises the federal government on drug and alcohol policies, and develops substance abuse prevention and education programs for youth. It publishes fact sheets, such as *Youth and Alcohol*, and pamphlets, such as *Who's Got the Power? You . . . or Drugs?*

National Institute on Alcoholism and Alcohol Abuse (NIAAA)
6000 Executive Blvd., Wilco Building
Bethesda, MD   20892-7003
Web site: www.niaaa.nih.gov

The NIAAA is one of the eighteen institutes that comprise the National Institutes of Health. NIAAA provides leadership in the national effort to reduce alcohol-related problems. NIAAA is an excellent source of information and publishes the quarterly bulletin, *Alcohol Alert*; a quarterly scientific journal, *Alcohol Research and Health*; and many pamphlets, brochures, and posters dealing with alcohol abuse and alcoholism. All of these publications, including NIAAA's congressional testimony, are available online.

Office for Substance Abuse Prevention (OSAP) National Clearinghouse for Alcohol and Drug Information (NCADI)
PO Box 2345, Rockville, MD   20847-2345
(800) 729-6686
Web site: www.health.org

OSAP leads U.S. government efforts to prevent alcoholism and other drug problems among Americans. Through the NCADI, OSAP provides the public with a wide variety of information on alcoholism and other addictions. Its publications include the bimonthly *Prevention Pipeline*, the fact sheet *Alcohol Alert*, monographs such as "Social Marketing/Media Advocacy" and "Advertising and Alcohol," brochures, pamphlets, videotapes, and posters. Publications in Spanish are also available.

Secular Organizations for Sobriety (SOS)
PO Box 5, Buffalo, NY   14215
(716) 834-2922
Web site: www.secularsobriety.org

SOS is a network of groups dedicated to helping individuals achieve and maintain sobriety. The organization believes that alcoholics can best recover by rationally choosing to make sobriety rather than alcohol a priority. Most members of SOS reject the spiritual basis of Alcoholics Anonymous and other similar self-help groups. SOS publishes the quarterly *SOS International Newsletter* and distributes the books *Unloaded: Staying Sober and Drug Free* and *How to Stay Sober: Recovery Without Religion*, written by SOS founder James Christopher.

Bibliography

Books

Anatoly Antoshechkin

Alcohol: Poison or Medicine? Bloomington, IN: First Books Library, 2002.

Douglas Beirness

Best Practices for Alcohol Interlock Programs, Ottawa, NE: Traffic Injury Research Foundation, 2001.

Rosalyn Carson-Dewitt, ed.

Encyclopedia of Drugs, Alcohol, and Addictive Behavior. New York: MacMillan Library Reference, 2001.

Carol Colleran and Debra Erickson Jay

Aging and Addiction: Helping Older Adults Overcome Alcohol or Medication Dependence. Center City, MN: Hazelden Information Education, 2002.

Griffiths Edwards

Alcohol: The World's Favorite Drug. New York: Thomas Dunne Books, 2002

Kathleen Whelen Fitzgerald

Alcoholism: The Genetic Inheritance. Friday Harbor, WA: Whales Tales, 2002.

Anne M. Fletcher

Sober for Good. Boston: Houghton Mifflin, 2001.

Gene Ford

The Science of Healthy Drinking. San Francisco: Wine Appreciation Guild, 2003.

Eric Newhouse   *Alcohol: Cradle to Grave*. Center City, MN: Hazelden Information Education, 2001.

Thomas Nordegren   *The A–Z Encyclopedia of Alcohol and Drug Abuse*. Parkland, FL: Brown Walker, 2002.

Heather Ogilvie et al.   *Alternatives to Abstinence: A New Look at Alcoholism and Choices in Treatment*. Long Island City, NY: Hatherleigh, 2001.

Nancy Olson   *With a Lot of Help from Our Friends: The Politics of Alcoholism*. New York: Writers Club, 2003.

David Paciocco   *Canada's Blood Alcohol Laws: An International Perspective*, Ottawa, ON: Canada Safety Council, 2002.

J. Vincent Peterson et al.   *A Nation Under the Influence: America's Addiction to Alcohol*. Boston: Allyn and Bacon, 2002.

Frederick Rotgers et al.   *Responsible Drinking: A Moderation Management Approach for Problem Drinkers*. Oakland, CA: New Harbinger, 2002.

Lori Rotskoff   *Love on the Rocks: Men, Women, and Alcohol in Post-World War II America*. Chapel Hill: University of North Carolina Press, 2002.

Joseph Santoro et al.   *Kill the Craving: How to Control the Impulse to Use Drugs and Alcohol*. Oakland, CA: New Harbinger, 2001.

Periodicals

Jennifer Butters et al.   "Illicit Drug Use, Alcohol Use and Problem Drinking Among Infrequent and Frequent Road Ragers," *Drug and Alcohol Dependence*, 2005.

Polly Curtis   "Alcohol at Home Can Cut Teenage Binge Drinking, Study Says," *Society-Guardian* (United Kingdom), May 11, 2007.

Danielle Dick and Tatiana Foroud   "Candidate Genes for Alcohol Dependence: A Review of Genetic Evidence from Human Studies," *Alcoholism: Clinical & Experimental Research*, May 2003.

Donald Dougherty et al.   "Age at First Drink Relates to Behavioral Measures of Impulsivity: The Immediate and Delayed Memory Tasks," *Alcoholism: Clinical & Experimental Research*, March 2004.

Kristie Long Foley et al.   "Adults' Approval and Adolescents" Alcohol Use. *Journal of Adolescent Health*, 2004.

Alicia Justus et al.   "P300, Disinhibited Personality, and Early-Onset Alcohol Problems," *Alcoholism: Clinical & Experimental Research*, October 2001.

Robert Mann et al.   "Alcohol Consumption and Problems Among Road Rage Victims and Perpetrators," *Journal of Studies on Alcohol*, 2004.

Robert Mann et al.   "Drinking-Driving Fatalities and Consumption of Beer, Wine and Spirits," *Drug and Alcohol Review*, 2006.

Robert Mann et al.   "The Effects of Drinking-Driving Laws: A Test of the Differential Deterrence Hypothesis," *Addiction*, 2003.

Matt McGue et al.   "Origins and Consequences of Age at First Drink. I. Associations with Substance-Use Disorders, Disinhibitory Behavior and Psychopathology, and P3 Amblitude," *Alcoholism: Clinical and Experimental Research*, 2001.

Iain O'Neil   "Teenagers Who Drink with Their Parents Are Less Likely to Binge Drink, According to a Study of 10,000 Children," *Morning Advertiser* (United Kingdom), May 11, 2007.

Irving Rootman et al.   "Predictors of Completion Status in a Remedial Program for Male Convicted Drinking Drivers," *Journal of Studies on Alcohol*, 2005.

Maria Wong et al.   "Behavioral Control and Resiliency in the Onset of Alcohol and Illicit Drug Use: A Prospective Study from Preschool to Adolescence," *Child Development*, 2006.

Andrew Woodcock   "Alcohol at Home Could Help Cut Teenage Binge Drinking," *Scotsman* (Scotland), May 12, 2007.

Index